Who Shall Live?

A Report Prepared for the American Friends Service Committee

WHO SHALL LIVE?

Man's Control over Birth and Death

HQ
766.3
F7

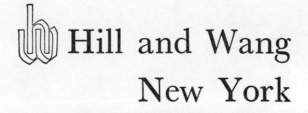 Hill and Wang
New York

At its meeting on October 31, 1969, the Board of Directors of the American Friends Service Committee, mindful that it does not speak for all Friends, endorsed the general point of view embodied in this report. The Board authorized the publication of this study, in the belief that it may contribute helpfully to the current dialogue on the subjects with which the report deals.

GILBERT F. WHITE, *Chairman*
Board of Directors
American Friends Service Committee

Contents

Preface

PUBLIC CONCERN over abortion and its role in society has led the American Friends Service Committee to consider what contribution the thoughts and beliefs of the Society of Friends (Quakers) might make to the resolution of the problem. As a result, the Family Planning Committee of the AFSC, in December 1966, appointed a Working Party to explore the issues involved in abortion and to prepare a report to the Board of Directors of the American Friends Service Committee.

The active interest of the AFSC in family planning dates back to 1935 and work among unemployed coal miners in West Virginia. Over the years since then family planning efforts have been included in the community development programs of the Service Committee in various parts of the world.

The assignment of our Working Party began as an exploration of the implications of abortion from the Quaker point of view. In our first meeting it became apparent that we could not consider the implications of abortion apart from our con-

vii

cern for the quality of life of the individual, the family, and society. Nor could we deal adequately with these subjects without taking into account contraception, sexual morality, and the role of genetic counseling in family planning. And finally, since the quality of life is affected by scientific advances in lengthening life, and since some of the same moral considerations apply to the control of birth and of death, we felt we must also explore the ethical issues implicit in the current concentration on prolonging the life of the dying. Thus, the study that began with abortion broadened and deepened to include exploration of the religious and moral issues posed by scientific advances in the control of death as well as in the control of birth.

This report is the result of our deliberations. It leaves unanswered many of the questions we raised. It does not presume to speak for all Quakers, whose views on the issues we considered are probably as varied as those of the public at large. We present it to the American Friends Service Committee simply as the thinking of concerned individuals who approached the assignment from a background of professional experience and of association with the Committee and with Quaker beliefs and practices. If our effort encourages Friends and others to ponder these matters and to arrive at guidelines for their own conduct, we shall consider our job well done.

Staff Writers	Members of the Working Party
JULIA ABRAHAMSON	HENRY J. CADBURY, Ph.D.
HARRY ABRAHAMSON	LORRAINE K. CLEVELAND, M.S.W.
	JOHN C. COBB, M.D., M.P.H.
Research Assistant	ELIZABETH C. CORKEY, M.D., M.P.H.
HELEN L. JENNINGS	RICHARD L. DAY, M.D.
	JOHAN W. ELIOT, M.D., M.P.H.
	J. RUSSELL ELKINTON, M.D.
	JOSEPH STOKES, JR., M.D.

Acknowledgments

THE WORKING PARTY wishes to acknowledge the great amount of help it has received in the preparation of this "statement" that has become a book. We have turned, in the various stages of preparation, to many people within and without the Society of Friends for information, for criticism, for wisdom.

In the field of religion and moral philosophy, we thank the following Quaker scholars: James F. Childress, Department of Religious Studies, University of Virginia; Wilmer Cooper, Dean, Earlham School of Religion, Earlham College; Christine R. Downing, Assistant Professor of Religion, Douglas College, Rutgers University; T. Canby Jones, Professor of Religion and Philosophy, Wilmington College; J. Floyd Moore, Professor of Biblical Literature and Religion, Guilford College; Douglas V. Steere, Emeritus Professor of Philosophy, Haverford College.

We have been assisted in the areas of demography, genetics, and reproduction by, and express our gratitude specifically to: William L. Brown, plant geneticist, Vice President and Di-

ix

rector of Research, Pioneer Hi-Bred Corn Company; James F. Crow, Professor of Medical Genetics, University of Wisconsin; Lincoln H. Day, Associate Professor of Public Health and Sociology, Yale University School of Medicine; Robert E. Hall, M.D., President, Jimmye Kimmey, Executive Director, and Cyril C. Means, Jr., Esq., member of the Board of Directors, all of the Association for the Study of Abortion; Luigi Mastroianni, Jr., M.D., Professor and Chairman of the Department of Obstetrics and Gynecology, University of Pennsylvania; Sheldon J. Segal, Director, Bio-Medical Division of the Population Council; William H. Telfer, Professor of Biology, University of Pennsylvania.

Helpful advice and encouragement have been received from the following Quaker physicians who, in addition to two members of the Working Party, have all served as Chairman of the Friends Medical Society: George A. Perera, M.D., Professor of Medicine and Associate Dean, Columbia University College of Physicians and Surgeons; Jonathan E. Rhoads, M.D., John Rhea Barton Professor and Chairman of the Department of Surgery, University of Pennsylvania; and J. Huston Westover, M.D., Acton Medical Associates, Acton, Massachusetts.

To one Quaker judge and member of the legal profession who for judicial reasons wishes to remain anonymous, we are grateful for his wisdom and participation in some of our discussions. Likewise we appreciate the critical encouragement of the members of our parent Family Planning Committee of the AFSC.

To the many members of the office staff of the American Friends Service Committee we are indebted for long hours of transcription of tapes and of letter writing, for organizational and administrative suggestions, and not least for substantive contributions to our thinking as it progressed.

Julia and Harry Abrahamson are listed in the front of this book as "staff writers." Let there be no mistake: they wrote this book as it now stands. Participants rather than ghost writers, the Abrahamsons took the transcriptions of our five working conferences, the heatedly debated composite statements, and the many individually written position papers, digested them, and melded them into one flowing, unified form. Furthermore, in so doing, they expressed the consensus of the Working Party in a manner that brought the Party's unanimous approval.

Finally, let us acknowledge the contributions of the wives and husbands of the members of the Working Party. They have shown forbearance and given encouragement; they are the spouses who have spiced our thinking with that priceless combination of common sense, plain speaking, and loving comradeship that lies at the center of the family life whose quality is the chief concern of this book.

The Working Party

Introduction

FOR THREE HUNDRED YEARS members of the Society of Friends (Quakers) have been seekers after truth. Believing in the continuing revelation of truth, they have tried to apply past experience and new knowledge to the search for moral solutions to contemporary problems.

The belief that the Supreme Power in the universe is good and that every human being has within him an innate quality which responds to goodness has led Quakers to try to cultivate this quality in order that all men may realize their potential in creative, satisfying, and mutually beneficial lives.

The best known and broadest concerns of Friends, expressed in their testimony against war and capital punishment, have been based on this reverence for the human personality and concern for the quality of men's lives. So have other efforts of Quakers through the years: efforts to free the slaves, to reform prisons and mental institutions, to heal the wounds of war, to feed the starving, to rehabilitate the victims of man's cruelty, to build bridges of understanding between peoples.

Today all men face threats to the quality of their lives un-dreamed of three centuries ago. In the years since 1652, when the Society of Friends came into being, the rise of modern science has led to a radical change in man's view of himself in the universe. Where once he thought of himself as created only a few thousand years ago, he now knows he is part of an evolutionary process that has been going on for billions of years. In that process he has arrived at a stage of knowledge and technology whereby he himself has the power, at least in part, to determine the direction in which he will evolve in the future. Recent discoveries in biology and genetics have given man far greater control over life than ever before.

Science has also given man power to alter his environment, to modify his physical health, to eliminate some of his genetic defects, to lengthen his life, to free himself from want—if he will—and, at the same time, to threaten the very survival of his species through nuclear war, environmental pollution, and overpopulation.

The impact of scientific knowledge on human life has cre-ated a new urgency and an inescapable obligation to weigh very carefully the choices we make from now on, the priorities we set for the use of our powers and our resources. Indeed, if man is to have a future at all, we are *forced* to think of the choices open to us. These are difficult and painful, for they affect not only the beginning and end of human life but the quality of life in all the years that lie between.

Friends have addressed themselves repeatedly to issues in-volved in war and the arms race and have tried to present constructive moral alternatives. They have had limited occa-sion in the past to develop any specific attitudes toward the population problem and abortion, questions that are now agitating the public mind and conscience. The decision to ex-plore the moral issues posed by scientific advances in the con-trol of birth and death stems from the experience of the American Friends Service Committee in its efforts to express a Quaker concern for human welfare. This experience has brought the realization that it is impossible to improve the quality of life for people throughout the world without addressing ourselves to the problem of overpopulation with its tragic results of poverty, ignorance, malnutrition, and disease. Nor is peace possible when millions of people—hungry, homeless, without hope—drag themselves through lives of desperation.

In its study, the Working Party of the Service Committee reviewed the accomplishments of medical and biological science and the prospect of further advances in the control of life and death. These add up to an impressive list of what man *can* do. Our main task was to try to think through what man *ought* to do in the face of the tremendous problems he has created.

Chapter 1

The Population Problem

IN DECEMBER 1968 man got his first look at his world from outer space. Incredible that 3.5 billion people should be living on that small spinning planet! That over a million more are arriving each week is even more staggering. How can our finite globe, with its limited resources, supply the essentials so many billions of people need to sustain life and to grow in mind and spirit?

The answer is that it cannot. Half the people of the world are already hungry. But if we do not control our fertility, in less than thirty-five years there will be twice as many people on earth. This prospect is as great a threat to the future of society as the arms race and nuclear war.

The Problem Now

Our predicament is the result of man's achievement in the conquest of death. For thousands of years high birth rates were canceled by high death rates. This balance no longer exists, not because the birth rate has gone up but because the death rate has gone down. Many of the former causes of death have been conquered by advances in technology and biomedical science. Whereas millions of babies once died at birth or in infancy, the majority now live to produce children of their own, who in turn survive through their reproductive years. By 1969 the estimated death rates had been reduced to a world average of 15 per thousand, compared to the 35 to 45 per thousand common in earlier years.

Since World War II the reduction in mortality has been rapid in the less developed countries. After an extensive public health campaign in Ceylon, the death rate fell 30 per cent in a single year. In India today eighty out of one hundred babies live to reproductive age; not long ago less than half that number survived to the age of twenty. In some parts of the world (Ceylon, Malaysia, Taiwan), the death rate is lower than the 9.6 per thousand of the United States, primarily because the population is younger.

The birth rate has not experienced a corresponding decline. It has declined in the Western nations and Japan but continues to be high in the poorer, developing countries. The United States birth rate in recent years has fluctuated between 18.4 per thousand in 1933 and 25.3 in 1957. The mid-1969 estimate was 17.4, according to the Population Reference Bureau. Birth rates in developing countries range from 35 to over 50 per thousand; the world average is 34.

The population is growing most rapidly in the developing countries, where two thirds of the world's people now live. Their rate of growth (2 to 3.8 per cent a year) is two to five times higher than that of Europe (.8 per cent), the United States (1 per cent), and the Soviet Union (1 per cent).*

This population growth has wiped out gains in food production. In spite of a 32 per cent increase in the production of food between 1955 and 1965, the developing countries,

* See Appendix I, Table 1, for information on population growth.

which once had grain surpluses for export, do not now produce enough food to feed themselves nor enough other products to buy the food they need. As a result, the population of half the world exists on the edge of starvation. It is estimated that about ten thousand people die every day as the result of malnutrition. Many of those who do not die are condemned by lack of adequate food to live permanently fatigued, stunted in growth, vulnerable to disease, listless, apathetic, unable to contribute to their own or their country's well-being.

The increasing demands of a constantly growing population make it difficult even to maintain the inadequate standards of the past, much less to save for the future. Economic progress is difficult, sometimes impossible. A higher rate of population growth calls for more capital to provide necessary facilities and services. But in the poorer countries the yearly increase in the gross national product is often only 2 per cent, compared to a rate of about 4 per cent in industrial nations. Not only food production but all of the factors involved in the standard of living show similar trends. Thus, governments that have been trying to improve the lives of their people often find their efforts doomed by the ever greater number who need food, clothing, housing, schooling, health services, and jobs.

The extreme youth of the population adds a further dimension to the problem. In the developing countries 40 to 50 per cent are under fifteen years of age (compared to 30 per cent in the United States and 21 per cent in Sweden): too young to contribute to the economy but with mouths to feed, bodies to clothe, and minds to educate. And how are the young to be trained for jobs, which in any case are limited or nonexistent because of lack of capital for industrial and agricultural development?

Much of the world's unrest and tension can be traced to the poverty and deprivation of half the world's people, to their rising expectations, and to our inability to equate population and resources.

The United States also has a population problem. Its annual rate of growth is less than half that of most developing countries, and population density is not yet excessive. But in terms of opportunities for all of its people, the United States does have serious problems resulting from pressure of population on resources, from urbanization, from unequal distribution of the country's wealth, and from misuse of resources. Thirty million Americans are poor. They suffer from inadequate educational facilities, lack of medical care, often from unemployment; even, according to recent studies, from malnutrition. They may not starve, but many often go to bed hungry. A survey by the United States Department of Health, Education, and Welfare in the spring of 1969 revealed dietary deficiencies that shocked government nutritionists. Example: Among fifteen hundred children aged four to five in Head Start programs in Louisiana, Alabama, and Mississippi, 72 per cent were below normal in growth, and many were in need of medical treatment for anemia.

Rich or poor, all Americans are affected by population pressures. Such pressures are evident in overcrowded schools, deteriorated housing, spreading ghettos, the increasing cost of municipal services (garbage collection, fire and police protection, street cleaning, etc.), highways jammed with traffic, inadequate transportation, diminishing open space and land for recreation, and shortage of doctors, teachers, and welfare workers.

Population growth, together with technological progress and industrialization, has also led to the overuse and abuse of precious resources: land, air, water, forests, and animal life. We have steadily taken over more and more agricultural land for roads, housing, and industry. We have eroded and impoverished the soil through exploitation. We have destroyed our forests to provide space for expansion, wood for burning or building, paper for hundreds of purposes. We have polluted the air we breathe with noxious fumes from industrial plants, motor vehicles, airplanes, domestic heating, and the burning of litter. We have contaminated our rivers, lakes, and streams with wastes and synthetic detergents, poisoning fish and destroying precious food and recreational resources. We have been poisoning animals and birds with pesticides. With thoughtless profligacy, we have been using up such irreplaceable resources as coal, oil, and metals.

The Years Ahead

If the 2 per cent rate of population growth should continue, the population would double in thirty-five years. For every person in the world today there would be two to feed, clothe, house, and educate. Even to maintain our present inadequate standards, without providing for *any* improvement, we would have to grow twice as much food and to double all existing facilities—schools, housing, hospitals, health centers, factories, roads.

Developing countries would have twice as many people in a much shorter time span. Some of the Latin American countries, for example, would double their populations in twenty to twenty-four years. The food needs in developing nations will more than double in twenty years, according to the report of the Panel on the World Food Supply of the President's Science Advisory Committee, May 1967.

The predictions of experts on the outcome of the race between population and resources range from guarded optimism to despair.

Optimists call attention to the recent bumper crops in India and Pakistan, made possible by chemical fertilizers, the use of new high-yield strains of rice, wheat, and corn, and modern irrigation techniques. They emphasize the fact that these same practices are spreading to other developing nations. They point to the areas of uncultivated land, which with water and other investment could be made productive, and to the possibility of "farming" the oceans. They are encouraged because the richer nations are realizing increasingly that it is in their own self-interest to help the peoples of poorer countries toward a better life. They believe that the efforts already under way to control human fertility and to promote economic development will solve the problem.

Donald J. Bogue, University of Chicago sociologist, expects birth rates to drop sharply as contraceptives are widely accepted, with population growth stabilized at zero or near zero by the year 2000.

According to Gustav F. Papanek, an economist with Harvard University's Development Advisory Service, as people begin to be aware of the success of advances in public health, birth rates will decline. He states that as fewer children die, fewer will be born. "When people realize their children are not dying, the birth rate will go down."

Others view the future with alarm. They believe that the food supply cannot keep pace with the population increase. They point out that 80 per cent of the total world exports of food in 1965 came from Canada and the United States, that the formerly huge grain stocks in the United States have been all but exhausted, and that expanding needs in the more advanced countries will further reduce the fraction of world needs they can supply. They do not see much hope that the available land, nearly all of it marginal, can be made productive, because the cost would be prohibitive for poor countries, even with outside aid. Experts see no evidence that the necessary reduction in birth rate is occurring among the peoples of Africa, Asia, and Latin America.

Some authorities hold that the excess of births over deaths will become even greater because further improvement in public health measures is likely to come before the necessary reduction in births. Convinced that mass starvation is inevitable unless drastic action is taken without delay, they predict widespread famine within the next ten to twenty years.

According to Harrison Brown of the California Institute of Technology, the world food picture will not get better without massive technical assistance from the advanced nations. Major economic aid, he believes, must be combined with direct agricultural assistance and effective birth control measures.

Living space will also become a desperate problem in the years ahead, even in the United States, because of the inevitable urbanization of technically advanced countries. The population of the United States, by the year 2000, is expected to grow by another one hundred million people, most of whom will be crowded into urban centers that already hold 70 per cent of the population on less than 10 per cent of the nation's land. The prospect before the poorer, more crowded countries is much more appalling in terms of congestion and damage to the quality of life. Once it was possible to reduce population pressure on living space by emigration. Today few countries welcome immigrants, and only insignificantly small numbers of people find it possible to emigrate.

LaMont C. Cole, Professor of Ecology, warns that we may one day find ourselves short of breathable air because we remove huge quantities of oxygen from the air by burning oil, coal, and natural gas and, at the same time, prevent the production of oxygen by reducing the amount of land vegetation and by poisoning vegetable life (diatoms) in the sea, from which most of our oxygen comes.

Many demographers believe it is entirely possible that population pressures may cause a breakdown in man's physical and social health, in his capacity to organize society for effective use of the world's resources. This, they suggest, may stop population growth through revolution, famine, epidemic, and war long before we run out of food, space, and air. In testimony on the population crisis before the Senate Subcommittee on Foreign Aid Expenditures in 1968, Philip M. Hauser, University of Chicago demographer, said:

I am convinced that under the most optimistic assumptions that can be made with respect to fertility decline during the remainder of this century, the world is faced with prospects of more, not less, social unrest; with greater, not lesser, political instability; with greater, not fewer, threats to world peace; with intensified, not diminished, cold war and hot war.

The effect of overpopulation on the individual human spirit may be even more devastating than its physical results. In an impersonal, overcrowded world, what happens to man's dignity and self-respect, to his sense of importance and fulfillment?

Although experts differ on the dimensions of the population problem, all agree that it is serious. At the Second World Population Conference in 1965, experts presented evidence that: population would be more than six billion by the year 2000; death rates would continue to fall in developing areas, but birth rates might not fall for some time; food supplies might not keep pace with the ever-growing populations predicted for some areas; urban centers would grow, creating increasingly difficult problems of sanitation, housing, and transportation; natural raw materials would become scarcer because of the wastefulness of present use; mineral supplies might run out. They agreed, too, on the urgency of planned economic development.

Clearly, the quality of life for the world's billions, present and future, depends in large measure on our ability to balance population and resources. In the past, war, famine, and epidemic disease were important factors in maintaining such a balance. No one suggests that we should encourage wars or turn the clock back in our struggle against death-dealing epidemics and disease. Demographers and ecologists agree that if man is to restore the balance he has destroyed, we must reduce the birth rate significantly.

Chapter 2

Man's Control over Birth

PEOPLE HAVE ALWAYS WANTED CHILDREN—but not in unlimited numbers. In the introduction to *Medical History of Contraception*, Norman E. Himes stated that "Men and women have always longed for both fertility and sterility, each at its appointed time and in its chosen circumstances. *This has been a universal aim, whether people have always been conscious of it or not.*"

In early societies unwanted children were often disposed of after they were born. Infanticide was common: Sometimes babies were killed outright, sometimes abandoned to the elements. Christians have always rejected infanticide, but the church inadvertently facilitated abandonment by providing places designed so that infants could be left without identification of the mother.

Contraception

The wish to prevent births goes back at least several thousand years. Contraception has existed in some form

9

through all of social evolution. Coitus interruptus was known and practiced in preliterate societies, but since most people did not understand the physiology of conception and reproduction, contraceptive methods were generally more magical than scientific. Primitive African women drank potions of herbs, leaves, or various obnoxious substances; ate a castor bean once a year; applied mixtures or materials internally; underwent rites conducted by medicine men; tied magic knots. Other cultures added the use of charms and amulets, medicated pessaries, sticky substances applied to the genitals.

Evidence about the practice of contraception in China is rare, but contraceptive recipes appear in Chinese medical texts in the form of prescriptions quoted from the *Ch'ien chin fang* by Sun Ssu-mo, who died in A.D. 695. Contraception was also practiced in other Asian cultures; in Egypt, where contraceptive prescriptions found on papyrus date back to 1850 B.C.; in the civilizations of the ancient Jews, Greeks, and Romans; and in the Islamic world and medieval Europe.

As medical and biological information increased, contraceptives became more effective, but it was not until the nineteenth century that fairly reliable contraceptive knowledge became more widely available, primarily in Western societies and especially in England, Germany, and France.

The beginning of the birth control movement can be traced to Francis Place, an early nineteenth-century social reformer, who, in a pamphlet printed in 1822, made an attempt to educate the masses in the need for contraception. Applying the population theories of Malthus to the daily lives of individuals, he tried to inform workingmen of the social and economic advantages of contraception in preventing poverty and raising the standard of living. Others who followed him (Robert Dale Owen, Charles Knowlton, Dr. C. R. Drysdale, Annie Besant, Marie Stopes, and, in the United States, Margaret Sanger) suggested specific methods, gave wide publicity to the need for contraception, founded birth control clinics in various parts of the world, and sometimes suffered raids and imprisonment for their efforts.

Today the birth control movement, now referred to as "planned parenthood" or "family planning," has spread to many countries of the world. Its goal—limiting a family's children to the number parents can care for comfortably—has been accepted by most religious groups, by physicians, by social thinkers, and by many of the world's leaders. Information on contraceptive methods* can be obtained through private agencies and through an increasing number of official government programs.

By 1967, in addition to services made available by scores of privately financed clinics in the United States, forty-four states had at least one health unit providing family planning services, and the welfare departments in thirty-four states paid the costs of such services. Yet neither these programs nor those in other countries have been conspicuously successful in reducing the birth rate.

After fifteen years of a national policy of family planning in India, the birth rate has not significantly declined. Voluntary organizations have programs in more than one hundred countries, but to date encouraging progress in bringing down birth rates has occurred only in Taiwan, Hong Kong, and Singapore. Birth rates even in these countries had begun to fall before large-scale family planning programs were initiated, primarily because of other factors, including rising standards of living and of education and the age structure of the population.

In recent years, the governments of some of the developing countries—most notably India—have been offering incentives to encourage sterilization of parents with three or more children.

In one way or another, much of the world is beginning to struggle to limit population. The results so far have not been notable. Formidable barriers still stand in the way of universal use of contraceptives.

Great emphasis is placed on the importance of childbear-

* For a description of methods of contraception, their effects and effectiveness, see Appendix III.

ing in most cultures and religions, especially in developing countries. In earlier times, a society's survival depended on a high birth rate. Children were needed to work in the fields, to care for parents in their old age, as well as to perform religious rituals and to carry on family tradition. Parents had to have a number of children because so many of them died. Too many still die. But in many areas popular attitudes toward family size have not yet adjusted to the fact that the large families of former times are no longer necessary.

Many couples still want more than three children, which would result in a population larger than the world can sustain. This means that even if everyone had access to contraceptives, the birth rate would not decline sufficiently to achieve a stationary population.

The population problem is further complicated by the fact that often couples have more children than they want or can care for. According to a 1965 poll reported by N. B. Ryder and C. F. Westoff, 21 per cent of the women in the United States who were sampled acknowledged that at least one of their children was unwanted.

The opposition to family planning programs on the part of certain governments, religious groups, and special interests continues to be a deterrent to birth control. Some groups hold to the belief, which others consider false in a technological age, that a large population makes a nation strong. They also insist that an expanding population, by providing larger markets for goods, is essential for economic development. There is evidence to the contrary in the examples of Japan and northern Europe, which are growing most slowly in population yet are among the world's most prosperous nations. The opposition of such groups, however, is not so powerful a deterrent as it once was. Many individuals today practice contraception in spite of prohibitions by the laws of their country or the teachings of their religion or both.

Although there are no longer any legal bans on the use of contraceptives in the United States, other legal restrictions often make them difficult to get. In many states restrictive legislation inhibits advertising of contraceptives in mail-order catalogues, magazines, newspapers, radio, television, etc.; prevents their display in pharmacies; and frequently prevents the sale of nonprescription contraceptives except by registered pharmacists and physicians. Local ordinances in some areas prohibit the sale of condoms in vending machines. Thus, the cost of getting medical advice and contraceptives, as well as not knowing where to get them, effectively militates against their use by the most vulnerable groups in the population—the poor, the young, and the unmarried.

A serious obstacle to the use of contraceptives is that it demands the need to plan, a concept foreign to many peoples. The change in values, attitudes, motivation, and incentive that must precede such planning cannot ordinarily be expected within less than a generation.

Another difficult hurdle, particularly where populations are largely rural, illiterate, and poor, is lack of adequate personnel and funds to spread information about family planning, to provide contraceptive materials, and to teach their proper use. In the United States, where it is estimated that more than five million low-income women need birth control help, about four out of five still have had no medical advice on how to limit the size of their families.

Even if such help were available free to the entire population, rich and poor alike, this alone would not solve the population problem. There is no conclusive evidence that universal access to information, supplies, and services would in itself bring the birth rate into balance with the death rate. Nor is propaganda exhorting people to have fewer children because of national or world population problems any more effective.

An essential factor in limiting births is motivation. Only the developed nations have had a marked decline in the birth rate, with the decline most evident among the well-educated, more financially secure families, whose children have a chance through education to achieve a better life. In recent years, however, there has been a trend toward equalization of birth rates among rich and poor.

All of the countries that have illiteracy rates above 50 per cent have birth rates ranging from 35 to over 50 per thousand; in most countries where illiteracy is below 10 per cent, birth rates are under 20 per thousand. Extensive use of birth control methods appears to come with rising aspirations, which are tied to improved education and a rise in standard of living. Experience has shown that parents limit their families for economic reasons and because they want to give maximum opportunities to their children. Many people in developing countries lack these incentives; they do not expect to become literate or prosperous in the foreseeable future. It is unrealistic, therefore, to expect birth control programs to be successful unless they go hand in hand with improved economic and cultural conditions.

Abortion

Motivation to prevent a birth, often nonexistent before the sexual act, is very high when a pregnancy is actually established. Abortion is the most widespread method of fertility control in the world. It is also the most furtive. Roughly twenty-five to thirty million women have induced abortions each year; the vast majority are performed outside hospitals.

It is estimated that for every woman in the United States who is hospitalized for a therapeutic or legal abortion (approximately eight thousand to ten thousand a year), one hundred other women either go to a criminal abortionist or operate on themselves. This estimate does not include the number of women who are affluent enough to travel to other countries for help. In most of western Europe the illegal abortion rate is believed to be higher than that in the United States; it is higher still in Latin American countries and others with restrictive legislation and small or nonexistent birth control programs.

In recent years the problem of abortion has been causing increasing concern. It is provoking intense public debate and world-wide controversy. Religious groups, governmental bodies, social agencies, and professional associations are examining every aspect of the subject—legal, social, medical, biological, humanitarian, religious, ethical, moral, political. The cases for and against abortion appear often in the popular press as well as in learned journals; abortion is debated from public platforms, in a fast-growing collection of books and papers, and over radio and television. A wide variety of agencies is producing and publicizing official position papers.* The experiences of several countries with legalized abortion and the contemplated revision of abortion laws by a number of states are spurring this upsurge of public interest and concern.

There are compelling reasons for the present searching inquiry. More and more people are alarmed at the extent of self-induced and criminal abortions and their cost in human life and suffering. Such abortions are an important cause of maternal deaths, and the number is growing. Adequate statistics on the injury to health are not available; and it is impossible to measure the fear and anguish that drive women to such acts.

While many illegal abortions are performed by physicians, too often women go to doctors who are no longer in good standing (because of alcoholism, drug addiction, other reasons) or to dangerous amateurs with no training in medicine. A survey in a small southern city, reported by sociologist Kenneth R. Whittemore, found that one of the city's five abortionists was a doctor dissatisfied with his profession; the others were a chiropractor, an antique dealer, a midwife, and a mechanic. Sometimes the abortionist has a well-equipped

* Selections are given in Appendix IV.

surgery where he operates in secret, but too often women must find their way down back alleys to dirty offices and submit to hurried operations performed without adequate precautions against infection; or they try to do it themselves. Some of these women described their agonizing search for help to Lawrence Lader, specialist in population problems, during his recent study of nonhospital abortions.

The chief victims are the poor. They have fewer abortions, legal and illegal, than the financially and educationally privileged because they are less likely to know how to go about getting one and less able to pay for it; frequently unable to pay even the fee of a medical quack, they more often operate on themselves; and, much more often, they die. The statistics are revealing. In New York City, four out of five therapeutic abortions over a twenty-year period were performed on white women who could afford the services of private physicians; almost 80 per cent of all abortion deaths occurred among nonwhite and Puerto Rican women.

The poor suffer more frequently than the privileged in still another way. Unable to get abortions or afraid to induce them, in many instances unaware of contraceptives or unable to get them and use them effectively, they simply continue to bear unwanted children.

The fate of the unwanted child is an important factor in the current inquiry into abortion. Judge Orman W. Ketcham of the Juvenile Court of the District of Columbia believes that "probably the major cause of our juvenile problem today is unwanted children." A Swedish study provides some information on what happens to unwanted children compared to average children. The study followed from birth to adulthood 120 children born to mothers whose requests for abortion had been refused, and compared them to wanted children born at the same time and carefully matched as to several family characteristics. The unwanted children were more often brought up in a broken home, more often registered for psychiatric services, more often registered for antisocial and criminal behavior, slightly more often cited for drunken conduct, and more often in need of public assistance than the wanted children. A few more of the unwanted were educationally subnormal, and far fewer pursued higher education. Unwanted boys were more often rejected for military service; girls more often married early and had children early. The authors conclude that in any application for legal abortion, the prospective child runs the risk of having to surmount greater social and mental handicaps than his peers, even when the grounds for the application are so slight that it is refused.

The flouting of abortion laws is a source of special worry to lawmakers, the legal profession, and enforcement agencies. They fear its possible impact on respect for all law, and they recognize that lack of enforcement has led to the organization of criminal abortion syndicates.

The current exploration has also been stimulated by new medical and biological knowledge about factors that may lead to the birth of a deformed or retarded child, and by new medical techniques that have reduced the risk of ending pregnancies.

One of the most compelling reasons for the present concern with abortion is the world population problem and the specter of spreading starvation, especially in the developing countries. The nations that permit abortions on request have experienced spectacular reductions in birth rates as well as in illegal abortions. In Hungary, the number of legal abortions exceeds the number of live births. Japan reduced its birth rate from over 34 per thousand to about 19, Rumania from 35.1 to 13.7. This last figure indicates a fertility rate below replacement level. The effectiveness of permissive abortion legislation in reducing birth rates has led to serious consideration of the role of such legislation as a backstop to failures in programs of contraception. Experience has shown that while liberal abortion policies produce a large initial increase in the reported abortion rate, over the years the trend appears to reverse as the use of contraceptives increases.

The fear in some quarters that legalized abortion or widespread use of contraceptives might result in an irreversible population decline has proved unfounded. When the government of Rumania, alarmed over the falling birth rate, reacted by providing special incentives for parenthood and placing strict limitations on abortion, the number of births promptly shot up to a new high of 38.4 per thousand. This sudden increase in the birth rate suggests the absence of effective methods of contraception. Where contraceptives are widely available and people are educated to their use, the birth rate goes up when couples decide they want more children and down when they do not. The experience of the United States proves this. During the Depression years, birth trends caused groundless fears of "race suicide"; but following World War II, more and earlier marriages, the earlier birth of the first child, and the birth of children postponed during the Depression led to a "baby boom."

Historical Background

Women have always practiced abortion or attempted it, in spite of taboos, laws, even the death penalty. The considerations that drove them to it in ancient times were probably very much the same as those motivating women today: poverty, illness, advanced age or extreme youth, the burden of too many children, the disgrace of bearing an illegitimate child, fear of discovery of infidelity, and numerous other social and psychological causes.

In an effort to end unwanted pregnancies, women in primitive societies thrust pointed objects into the uterus; applied hot coals to their bodies; jumped from high places; drank vile potions and purgatives; practiced magic rites. The use of mercury was advocated by a Chinese medical text said to be forty-six hundred years old. (The methods ignorant women use today are no less dangerous: the insertion of knitting needles, wire coat hangers, umbrella ribs; violent exercise; the use of soap solutions, pills, deadly chemicals.)

Attitudes on abortion varied as greatly in early cultures as

they do today, ranging from approval—even encouragement
—to absolute prohibition. Most of the Greek philosophers
approved of it. Aristotle considered it the best means of
keeping the population within acceptable limits. Plato, in
his ideal republic, urged it for women over forty. Roman
husbands could insist upon it. At the other extreme were
those who viewed abortion with abhorrence. In the Code
of the Assyrian Law relating to women, believed to have
been written in 1500 B.C., a woman who "causes to fall what
her womb holds . . . shall be tried, convicted, and impaled
upon a stake, and shall not be buried." The early Jews condemned abortion, and the early Christians equated it with
infanticide. The Roman theologian Tertullian, around A.D.
240, spoke of abortion as murder but apparently considered
it so only after the fetus had reached a certain age and
development.

In recent times, condemnation of abortion has centered
primarily around a view that holds to the inviolability of
the fetus. The first Christians considered abortion infanticide
because it was regarded as the killing of a developing human
being. Other theological authorities held that sometimes it
was murder and sometimes not, depending on the state of
development or formation of the fetus. The different views
were based on different opinions as to the point in the reproductive process when the fetus becomes infused with a
soul. That debate has gone on for nearly two thousand years.

The public conscience continues to be troubled, torn between concern for human welfare and the still unresolved
religious and ethical issues of when a new human life begins,
when the soul enters the body, and when, if ever, it is moral
to destroy a potential human being.

Biological Background

The biologist cannot pinpoint the exact moment when the
life of an individual begins. In his view life is continuous.
It exists in the sperm and the egg before conception; and

beginning with the fertilized egg, every stage in the reproductive process, as in the child, has potential for future
development.

To understand the legal, medical, and religious significance of the issues involved in abortion, it is necessary to
understand the various stages in the reproductive process.

The process begins when sperm cells, released in the vagina, pass up the uterus into the woman's Fallopian tubes.
The female egg cell, discharged by the woman's ovary once
a month, travels down the tube. If one of the sperm cells
penetrates the egg, fertilization occurs. The fertilized egg has
within it genetic information provided equally by sperm and
ovum.

For about three days the fertilized egg, called a zygote, remains in the Fallopian tube, dividing continuously. The resulting group of cells, in the form of a hollow ball (blastocyst),
is delivered to the uterus where it remains in the uterine fluid
until about one week after fertilization when it attaches itself
to the wall of the uterus, a process called implantation. (If it
fails to do so, menstruation occurs, and the blastocyst is eliminated.)

If all goes well, the blastocyst, which has become implanted
in the lining of the uterus, continues to grow. The outer
cells of the blastocyst form the fetal portion of the placenta,
through which the mother provides nourishment to the new
organism. By five weeks the basic organs develop.

By the end of the eighth week the skeleton has begun to
form, arms and legs develop, and complete organs begin to
take recognizable shape. At this point the fetus has acquired
much of its structure; from then on it simply grows and ma-
tures.

By twelve weeks the fetus is recognizably human. It can
move its arms and legs, though the mother is usually unaware
of this for an additional four to eight weeks.

"Quickening" occurs when the mother first feels the stirring
of her baby.

The twentieth week has special significance. Before that time the fetus is incapable of independent life; thereafter it has a bare chance for survival outside the womb. Such a birth, therefore, is no longer called a miscarriage or an abortion but a premature delivery, and in some jurisdictions it must be reported. (Modern British statute law considers the beginning of "viability"—the ability to survive outside the uterus—as twenty-eight weeks.)

Biology cannot say definitely at any one of these stages, nor at birth itself, "At this point a human life begins." Life is a continuum: Sperm and ovum are already living before fertilization; at the time of implantation a new embryo begins to grow, but this has no human appearance, form, or function; after a time the fetus becomes recognizably human; soon the fetus is capable of independent movement within the womb; after some further time (whose length has been shortened by the advance of medical knowledge and skills) the nervous system and other organs of the premature infant have matured sufficiently so that it is capable of life outside the uterus; at birth it must begin to breathe for itself and yet is still dependent on others for survival.

Biology, which discloses the secrets of the life process, also offers insights into the intricate systems of natural contraception and spontaneous abortion.

While Nature has provided a fantastic abundance of reproductive cells so that life will not die out, only a tiny fraction ever combine. Of the quarter of a billion sperm cells released with each ejaculation, only one is needed for fertilization; all of the other sperm die in a few hours or days. Only one of the ten to twelve eggs that partially mature every month in a woman's ovary is discharged, and that egg is capable of being fertilized for probably less than twenty-four hours. The union of sperm and egg depends, therefore, on correct timing.

If sperm and egg do manage to unite, Nature puts other obstacles in the path of the reproductive process. The fertilized egg has only about two out of three chances of continuing to divide on its journey down the Fallopian tube. Even if it reaches its destination, it may not succeed in implanting itself in the uterus.

Thereafter, primarily during the first three months of pregnancy, Nature corrects mistakes of lesser degree through spontaneous abortion of about one embryo in five. (Serious congenital defects are found in half or more of the fetuses that abort spontaneously, whereas surgical abortions reveal fetuses with a 5 per cent incidence of defect.)

Thus, only about half of all fertilized ova result in a live human being.

In earlier times, Nature provided for a further check on excessive population through the death of many babies shortly before birth and in the hours, days, and years after birth. Man has upset this balance by his successful fight against maternal and infant mortality. In the attempt to restore this balance, he has sought effective ways to reduce the number of lives that are started. Toward this end he has developed methods of preventing the union of sperm and egg or of preventing implantation.*

Man has also found safe ways of interrupting early pregnancies. There is little biological reason against his using them, at least sparingly, to remedy Nature's failures or to correct his own mistakes. But the biologist alone is not in a position to decide whether a potential life *should* be interrupted and, if so, when, under what circumstances, and how.

The Law and Abortion

In most of the United States the law still rules that pregnancy may not be interrupted, except to save a woman's life.

English Common Law, on which the first abortion laws in the United States were based, defined abortion as interrupting a pregnancy after quickening had occurred. The state laws enacted after the middle of the nineteenth century extended the definition of abortion to include pregnancy at any stage.

* See Appendix III.

These laws, however, do not equate the ending of pregnancy with the taking of human life after birth, for in most states the woman is not prosecuted, and the illegal abortionist is guilty of a felony, not of homicide, unless the woman dies as a result of the abortion.

Yet in certain respects the law still distinguishes between the state of the fetus before and after quickening. Many statutes impose more severe penalties for abortion after quickening. New York law still permits the execution of a pregnant woman under sentence of death if her fetus has not yet quickened; only if it has will she be reprieved. Setting this dividing line does not imply that the fetus is considered recognizably different the day after quickening from what it was the day before, just as the laws setting age limits for voting, marriage, driving, and financial responsibility do not contend that the person involved is any different the day after he reaches the given age. It is simply a legal recognition of the age-old and deep-seated human feeling that a fetus is not fully a human being before it moves and can live outside its mother.

Garrett Hardin, in an article in *ETC.* in 1967, likened an early embryo to a set of blueprints. The embryo contains specifications for a human being, but little human effort has been invested in it, and it can be repeated many times over if necessary. Therefore, our laws do not invest the embryo with the same value as an infant or an older child.

Most early state laws made abortion at any point a crime except where necessary to save a woman's life. Legislatures enacted these laws largely to prevent physical injury to women, since abortions in those days were dangerous, and to protect the public from the fraudulent and harmful substances widely sold as abortifacients before 1850. Other reasons for these restrictive laws have been advanced: to encourage population growth and to reflect recognition that quickening as a definition of human life is arbitrary and unscientific.

Over the past few years agitation for reform has resulted in some liberalization of abortion laws in the United States. By mid-1969, eleven states had modified their laws to include some or all of the following grounds for legal abortion: threat to physical or mental health, rape, incest, and potentially defective offspring.

The laws of other countries range from absolute prohibition to abortion on request.

Abortion is prohibited in all of Latin America, as in other Catholic lands, and in most Moslem countries. The Scandinavian countries and Iceland take into account a consideration absent from the most liberal state laws in the United States: the total life situation of the mother. England, liberalizing its law in October 1967, added other grounds: possible mental or physical injury to any of the existing children by reason of overcrowding, inadequate housing, strain on the mother, and other broad considerations. In Japan and the countries of eastern Europe, with the exception of East Germany and Albania, abortion has been permitted in recent years either on request or for a very wide range of conditions. Abortion, though formally illegal, is tolerated in Taiwan, South Korea, Israel, and some other countries.

Everywhere in the world, whether the laws prohibit or encourage abortions, women continue to have them. Even in Catholic countries, where religious as well as legal bans are absolute, estimates of the number of abortions are high: Brazil has an estimated 1,200,000 a year; Chile 125,000 to 150,000; Uruguay may have more abortions than live births; and the Catholic countries of Europe have many abortions.

Even where abortion is legal, women continue to seek illegal abortions—because their cases have been rejected, because of red tape and delay, or because they shy away from the public procedures involved before permission is granted.

State laws in the United States have been similarly ineffective. They are ignored by an estimated one million women annually, and by the hundreds of abortionists to whom these women turn for relief.

Many reputable physicians in leading hospitals, following established medical procedures, perform abortions if the woman's physical or mental health is endangered, if the woman is pregnant because of rape or incest, if there is a strong possibility that the child will be seriously deformed or retarded, or if the woman will be unable to care for the child for mental, physical, or social reasons. Yet in most states such abortions are of questionable legality or are clearly illegal. In states that permit abortions only to save the woman's life, hospital committees accept a psychiatrist's assertion that the operation is necessary to save the mother because of the risk of suicide. The majority of the therapeutic abortions in one major American city were performed for psychiatric reasons.

there still would be a possibility to put up the child for adopt.

In spite of the fact that such interpretations of the law are responsible for more abortions in hospitals than would otherwise be possible, and in spite of increased public interest in the problem of abortion, the number performed in hospitals in the United States has actually declined from thirty thousand annually twenty-five years ago to fewer than ten thousand today. Two reasons have been suggested. (1) Medical advances in the treatment of heart disease and other ailments have eliminated much of the risk to a woman's life, the sole consideration on which most states permit abortion. (2) Hospital abortion committees lack uniform standards, vary in decision-making procedures, and sometimes set up abortion quotas. Twenty-five years ago, the patient's physician simply consulted two medical colleagues, and if they agreed to end a pregnancy, it was done.

Prosecuting attorneys are reluctant to prosecute violations of the law for understandable reasons. In cases of hospital abortions they would be tangling with the leaders of the medical profession. In a number of states the prosecuting attorney would have to prove that the abortion was not performed in good faith to save the life of the woman. In cases handled by abortionists, two factors militate against the possibility of successful prosecution. (1) Most women will not testify against the person who helped them in a crisis. (2) Even if they would, in many jurisdictions prosecution cannot be based solely on the uncorroborated testimony of the woman, and there is seldom any witness to corroborate it. As a result, prosecution for illegal abortions is rare, even in the case of back-street operators, and convictions are even rarer.

Clearly, present laws do not reflect current medical knowledge and practice; neither do they reflect social attitudes. A survey conducted for the Population Council in 1967 revealed that a majority of people of all religious faiths believe abortion should be permitted in cases of rape and incest; 50 per cent of Catholics and a majority of those of other faiths approve abortion to prevent the birth of a deformed child.

Opponents of the present laws have argued that they are as unconstitutional and invalid as the Connecticut law against the prescription and use of contraceptives, which was struck down by the United States Supreme Court in 1965. They have pointed out that both the outlawed Connecticut statute and most abortion laws:

1. Seriously conflict with currently accepted standards of medical practice and science.
2. Invade intimate marital privacy.
3. Compel women to bear some abnormal children whose abnormality is predictable with a high degree of probability.
4. Are largely unenforced, but possible prosecution threatens the medical profession and inhibits development of publicly supported medical services.
5. Result in discrimination against the poor.
6. Interfere with limitation of numbers of children, thereby contributing to population pressures.
7. Involve imposition of the religious scruples of a portion of the community upon the entire community by government sanction.

Most of the present abortion laws are unconstitutional on other grounds as well, according to Professor Cyril C. Means, Jr., a legal historian and constitutional scholar. He points out that in the nineteenth century, when these laws were

passed, abortion—even in hospitals—was much more dangerous than childbirth, and that the original purpose of the
statutes was to compel women to adopt the safer of the two
alternatives. Since hospital abortions early in pregnancy are
much safer today than childbirth under the same hospital
conditions, the continued enforcement in the twentieth century of these nineteenth-century laws now frustrates their
original protective purpose by forcing women to accept the
less safe of the alternatives.

For a number of years critics of the present laws have
pressed for reform. In 1962 the American Law Institute,
after a ten-year study, approved a Model Penal Code intended
to serve as a blueprint for revision and reform of almost
every aspect of penal law. This code would legalize a hospital
abortion performed by a licensed physician if at least two
physicians certify in writing to the necessity of the abortion
on three principal grounds: (1) when there is "substantial
risk that continuance of the pregnancy would gravely impair
the physical or mental health of the mother"; (2) when there
is substantial risk "that the child would be born with grave
physical or mental defect"; (3) when "the pregnancy resulted
from rape, incest, or other felonious intercourse." *

In April 1967 Colorado became the first state to revise
its statute along these lines. By mid-1969 similar laws had
been passed in North Carolina, California, Maryland, Arkansas, Georgia, New Mexico, Kansas, Oregon, and Delaware.
(California does not permit abortion of potentially defective
children.) Mississippi modified its law only to the extent of
adding rape as grounds for abortion. In determining threat
to mental and physical health, Oregon's law takes into account the mother's total environment, "actual or reasonably
foreseeable." Maryland's law removes the performance of an
abortion by a licensed physician in a licensed hospital from
the criminal code and places it under the Medical Practices
Act. At this writing, bills to liberalize existing laws are under

* See Appendix V for excerpts from the Model Penal Code of the
American Law Institute.

consideration in more than half of all state legislatures. The proposed revisions are based largely on the American Law Institute model, but several newer bills remove abortion from the criminal code, as in the Maryland law.

Reactions to these proposals have been mixed, and the controversy continues. The suggested model statute of the American Law Institute is opposed by those who consider all abortion criminal and immoral and by those who want all abortion laws abolished on the grounds that state legislation in such matters is an invasion of privacy and of medical practice. It is defended because it is a realistic compromise between widely divergent views, the best that may be possible on an issue that arouses such intense feeling, and because the suggested conditions for legal abortion can most easily be justified on ethical grounds.

Analysts of the American Law Institute model point out what it would and would not do, if adopted.

It would legalize what is already current medical practice in the performance of therapeutic hospital abortions. It would remove the threat of criminal prosecution from physicians who perform them. It would also bring the law into conformity with moral views widely held by the public. And it would clarify some of the ambiguities in present laws, such as those that make unlawful abortion a crime but do not state what is unlawful.

The proposed reform would not significantly reduce illegal abortions nor the mortality from them, because the limited grounds on which abortions would be obtainable do not apply to most of the women who have them. According to Mrs. Peter Rossi, a University of Chicago sociologist, "Very few of the women who seek illegal abortions . . . fear a deformed fetus; few have serious heart or liver conditions; fewer still have been raped by a stranger or by their own father." Most abortions are sought by married women with children who do not want another child for social, economic, or personal reasons and by single girls and women who do not want to bear illegitimate children.

Adoption of the code would not help the poor, who are the chief victims of restrictions on abortion. It would not reduce the cost of legal abortions nor equalize opportunities to obtain them. It would not lead to improved law enforcement for the same reasons that violations are not now prosecuted.

Although the proposed code of the American Law Institute has been the center of most of the recent discussion and controversy, more liberal proposals are receiving increased attention. Some of these favor legislation that would permit abortion for social and economic conditions, as in the Scandinavian countries. Others advocate the more permissive legislation of eastern Europe, or simply the removal of all restrictions on the performance of abortions by licensed physicians in licensed and accredited hospitals.

All of the proposals for reform grow out of a commonly held conviction that the present laws are unsatisfactory, that they create more problems than they solve, and that some change is necessary. But legislators and members of the legal profession are as far from consensus on what ought to be done as other sections of the public. How greatly should the laws be liberalized, if at all? Is restrictive legislation a solution? Should abortion be a matter for criminal law? Should the law be involved at all? Will these questions become academic when the perfection of safe abortifacient pills makes the ending of pregnancy a purely private concern? Or should there then be laws prohibiting the manufacture and sale of such pills?

People need to be fully informed on the problems and questions, because in the end society must provide the answers.

The Physician and Abortion

Most doctors favor changing the abortion laws. A survey of over forty thousand physicians, by *Modern Medicine* in the spring of 1967, found 87 per cent favoring liberalization.

This is not surprising, for doctors are directly affected by these laws. Their experience points up reasons for advocating change.

Medically, hospital abortion presents little risk, especially during the first three months of pregnancy. The standard surgical technique is to stretch the opening of the womb with dilators and then remove the contents with special instruments. A newer method, developed in mainland China and now widely used, also before the twelfth week of pregnancy, takes a shorter time and further reduces risk and injury. A small tube with a hole near the end is inserted and cleans off the walls of the uterus through suction. After three months, doctors may use the salt solution method: The injection of a concentrated salt or sugar solution to replace the fluid around the fetus induces labor contractions in twenty to twenty-five hours, and the fetus is expelled. Or the physician may perform a miniature Caesarean operation (hysterotomy) by making a small incision in the uterus by way of the lower abdomen or the vagina and removing the fetus.

Death rates from legal abortions—particularly those performed before the twelfth week—are very low. In the United States it is safer to have a hospital abortion than to have a baby. The risks of abortion, according to Dr. Christopher Tietze, are one sixth to one tenth as dangerous as those attending pregnancy and childbirth. In 1964 Czechoslovakia reported no deaths in 140,000 abortions; Hungary two in 358,000. In recent years, mortality rates in eastern Europe have ranged from only one to four deaths per 100,000 legal abortions.

In contrast, the risk from illegal abortions is known to be very great, even though it is impossible to get accurate statistics on the number of deaths they cause or on the extent of permanent injury to women. In South America, where both the law and religion prohibit abortion, it is nevertheless the number one cause of death for women of childbearing age. From hospital records in the United States (and not all victims of self-induced or criminal abortion get to hospitals) an estimated four hundred to eight hundred women die each year from illegal operations. In New York City almost half of all deaths associated with childbearing are traced to these abortions; in ten years the death rate from this cause doubled.

To most doctors these are more than impersonal statistics. They have seen the victims in emergency rooms of hospitals; they have tried to save the lives of such women but, too often, have failed. Each case record recalls to some physician the suffering woman it describes.

Margaret S., 29 years old, mother of four, brought to the hospital three days after trying to induce abortion with a knitting needle. Severe hemorrhage. Died two days later in spite of massive blood transfusions.

Jean H., 42-year-old mother of five. Infection, the result of a soap solution injected by an abortionist four days before. Large doses of antibiotics administered. Died five days later.

One large municipal hospital in Boston admits an average of around six hundred victims of illegal abortion each year.

Another consideration that leads many doctors to advocate liberalization of abortion laws is their broadened view of the physician's calling. Medical practitioners in earlier days were concerned solely with curing disease and saving life. Modern physicians have added a new dimension: responsibility to promote and preserve health. Knowledge of the intimate relationship between mind and body and the physical impact of worry and stress has led the medical profession to think of health in new terms. Health is described by the World Health Organization as "a state of complete physical, mental, and social well-being, and not merely the absence of disease or infirmity." Doctors committed to such an interpretation often take into account, when considering a request for an abortion, not only whether the woman might die or suffer serious physical injury if her request is denied, but what the consequences would be in terms of her own and her family's well-being if they are forced to live in greater poverty, with a damaged or unwanted child, or with an illegitimate one.

Since most state legislation fails to define "health" when it is grounds for abortion at all, the laws often conflict with medical judgment and medical practice. The records of physicians disclose many requests for abortion on grounds that are of dubious legality. A few examples illustrate the doctor's dilemma.

The 40-year-old woman who is the sole support of her family since her husband's sudden incapacitating illness. What would they do if she could not work?

The 28-year-old mother of six, living with her family in overcrowded substandard housing, who begs for an abortion because there is no room for another child and she cannot take care of it.

A 17-year-old high school student, the only child of an invalid father and a working mother, who became hysterical on learning she was pregnant. "I *can't* have a baby," she cried. "My father and mother have sacrificed so much to give me an education. I can't tell them. It would kill them if I dropped out of school." She pleaded for help.

The patient who has already borne two defective children. If the doctor cannot assure her that the expected child will be normal, "he must not let it be born."

The patient of forty-seven with grown children, who had recently returned to a cherished career, interrupted years before for marriage and children; the family did not want another child; and at her age there was a great risk of producing a child with Mongolism. She is determined to have an abortion.

A young woman, pregnant as the result of extramarital intercourse after drinking too much at a party, told the doctor that her soldier husband, whom she loved dearly, had been in Vietnam for a year. "If you can't help me, I'll kill myself and my year-old baby."

Thousands of women for whom a particular pregnancy presents a similarly impossible social, economic, or psychological burden regularly appeal to qualified physicians for help. Since abortions for such reasons are not legal in most states, a doctor confronted with a case of this kind faces several distressing alternatives.

If the hospital in which he serves permits therapeutic abortions, he can tailor his recommendation for the abortion to fit legal specifications, falsifying the state of the woman's health or exaggerating the risk to her life. Should the hospital committee grant the request, they and he risk prosecution and possible imprisonment.

If his hospital does not sanction any abortions, or refuses to do so in this case, the doctor can decide to perform the operation secretly in his office, which is equipped only for minor surgery. In this case, too, he would be subject to imprisonment, and the woman to greater risk.

He might be able to refer the patient to a physician known to perform abortions, also a risky possibility. Or he might suggest that she go to another country where a safe abortion can be obtained, a course open only to the limited number who can afford the high cost of travel.

He can try to persuade the woman to carry the baby to term, in spite of the burden this would impose. If his plea succeeds, what would this mean to her and her family? Does he have the right to urge her to bring another unwanted child into the world? Should he encourage her to bear the child and place it for adoption with a couple who do want a baby?

Finally, the doctor can refuse to do anything, and this may be the most difficult choice of all for a man of conscience. To what lengths would this desperate woman go to end her pregnancy? Would she try to operate on herself? Would she seek relief in the dirty, back-alley room of a nonmedical abortionist? Would she arrive at the emergency room of a hospital, hemorrhaging, infected, perhaps dying because he had turned her away?

Another agonizing problem is whether or not to advise abortion where there is risk of a defective child. About one in fifty babies is born with some inherited defect. Among the many such defects is Mongolism (Down's syndrome), a condition that produces severe mental retardation. Retardation and serious defects may also result from German measles contracted early in pregnancy. Other defects (such as degenerative diseases of the nervous system) are produced by genetic difficulties caused by recessive genes—a one-in-four possibility when both parents are normal carriers of the causative gene.

It is now possible, in a few major medical centers, to diagnose certain illnesses of the fetus at or shortly after the twelfth week of pregnancy. Chemical tests performed on fluid withdrawn by a needle through the abdominal wall and the uterine wall of the pregnant woman can reveal the presence of abnormal substances or the absence of normal ones. This is a safe procedure, and the resulting diagnosis can, in certain instances, predict possible fetal damage with almost 100 per cent accuracy. Where diagnosis is certain, the ethical issues are clearer and the doctor's decision is easier. In most cases, however, there is uncertainty, and the decision must rest on probabilities. Where there is this uncertainty, should the physician advise abortion, risking the destruction of a normal fetus on the one-in-four chance that it might be abnormal or subnormal? If he advises against abortion and a seriously defective child results, what would this mean to the life of the child, the family, and society?

And what of the psychological effect on the woman if her request for an abortion is granted? Physicians know what the statistics say: that the majority of women do not feel guilty afterward; that a relatively small percentage are haunted by self-reproach; that far from causing psychiatric illness, abortion is often a defense against it. But how would this particular patient react? Would it help her or make her even more miserable?

Doctors have no common view on what should be done in any of the above cases. They share the dilemma of society. But none are more certain than physicians that something should be done about present abortion laws. All but a small minority favor liberalization, at least to the extent suggested by the American Law Institute.

Chapter 3

Religious and
Ethical Questions

THEOLOGIANS AND ETHICISTS are as divided on the profound issues posed by questions of abortion as the medical and legal professions and the general public. Friends have been similarly divided.

Individual Friends and groups of Friends are aware of the widespread reconsideration of traditional attitudes currently under way in the secular disciplines. They also share in the concern that is moving religious groups of our time to inquire afresh into the meaning of some of the issues affecting abortion, both as a moral question and as a theological question bearing on the sanctity of individual human life as derived from God.

To help interested Friends and others share with us in such an inquiry, we have set down some of the religious and ethical questions we have explored.*

* Our conclusions appear in Chapter 6.

The Issues

Is taking a human life ever justified? Is there an absolute standard against it?

Governments have justified killing human beings under certain circumstances. Although they prohibit murder, they have often sanctioned capital punishment and the destruction of life in war. The traditional attitude of Friends toward war and capital punishment seems to imply an absolute standard against the taking of human life.

How does this concern for the sanctity of life relate to abortion? What do we mean by a human life? At what point in the reproductive process does a human life begin? Is the embryo or fetus a person?

Theologians and others have debated these questions for centuries. Many cultures, especially Far Eastern ones, have set birth as the beginning of a human life. The Greeks and most medieval theologians chose an intermediate stage in the development of the fetus. This view continues to be widespread, with quickening often designated as the crucial time. Some question whether a human life can be said to begin before the brain becomes active.

Theologians seem to be saying that the fetus is and is not a human being; that it is human only potentially, but that this potential is very precious; and that indeed all of us are only potentially fully human. They hold that our unique and sacred value is not in something we have in ourselves, but only in our relation to God's purpose and his valuing of us. To the Scholastics a fetus was potentially a human person before the infusion of the rational soul. The point at which the developing fetus was considered an actual human being was the moment it was animated, which meant "given an *anima,* or spirit." According to the Old Testament, this happens at birth, when God breathes his spirit into man. Until 1869 the Roman Catholic Church tended to accept the Aristotelian interpretation that the soul of a male child was infused forty days after conception; that of a female child, eighty days. Where it was impossible to determine the sex of the abortus, it was presumed to have been female. Therefore, abortion during the eighty-day period was not considered homicide. Since 1869, many Catholic theologians have held that ensoulment may take place as early as conception, but they have never reached consensus on the precise moment this occurs, and no dogma has been promulgated. In her legislation, however, the Church assumes that animation takes place at conception.

Friends have not participated in this theological debate. Historically they have been concerned with the sanctity of human life, but they have not felt it necessary to pinpoint the beginning of a human life. Does it begin before one is self-conscious, before one can think and relate to others? If not, the dividing line certainly comes after birth, and refinements of dating prior to birth are irrelevant to abortion.

If questions of when a human life begins and when the fetus has a soul cannot be determined with precision, and if the chief consideration is concern for the potential of the fetus, we must ask ourselves how much we value that potential. Do we value it so much that we believe the fetus has an absolute right to life?

The traditional answer of the Catholic Church has been that potential human life must be protected at all costs. This position is based on the belief that man is created in the image of God; it guards against actions that threaten this divine potential, actions that might stem from any of a multitude of human weaknesses, such as sexual license, selfishness, and irresponsibility; it refuses to delegate to any individual God's right to decide who shall live. Protagonists for this point of view emphasize the defenselessness of the unborn child, its need for protection, its absolute right to life because of its potential humanity. They hold that abortion violates the profoundly held religious conviction that every human life deserves respect and reverence.

A number of present-day theologians and moral philosophers question these assumptions. They ask whether equal
reverence must be accorded to potential and actual human
life. Even if the fetus is a potential human being, they are
not prepared to confer absolute value upon it.

What if the fulfillment of the potential of the fetus is
menaced by factors threatening its physical or mental health
and development? What lies ahead for the unwanted child?
How do we balance a child's right to be born against its
right to a decent life? By preoccupation with the potential
of the unborn child, are we ignoring attention to the ethical
responsibility concerned with the quality of its life after
birth?

And what of the mother, the family, and society? Is it
morally right to expect a woman to bear a child against her
will? What if the pregnancy is the result of rape? Should a
woman be forced to bring into the world a child she cannot
or will not care for? What if its birth threatens her physical
or mental health and therefore her potential as a mother
and a human being? What moral weight should be given to
the effect of the birth on the family and society? By what
guides do we choose between the potential of the unborn
child and the potentials of others already living or still to be
born?

These moral issues relate directly to questions inherent in
present legal obstacles to contraception and abortion and
to proposed legal reforms. Should the reduction of unwanted
pregnancies be encouraged by freer access to contraceptives?
Would the wider availability of contraceptives and/or the
liberalization of abortion laws stimulate sexual promiscuity?
Is opposition to reform based more on fear of sexual irresponsibility and license than on legal concern to protect human
life? If so, is it right to use the law to enforce morality?
Should everything that may be ethically wrong be legally
prohibited? Should legal reform be supported because of

evils it may correct even if some of its results cannot be justified morally?

Questions concerned with the world and the future of man also press urgently for examination. In view of the threat of overpopulation, what is our moral responsibility for the survival and well-being of society? Does it demand that we limit the size of our families, by use of contraceptives if possible, by abortion if necessary?

Is it enough to limit births only to those babies who are wanted? The answer of the United Nations, implicit in its Declaration of Human Rights, and of many religious groups, including Quakers, would be an unqualified "Yes." Yet many families throughout the world, including highly educated, well-to-do couples (Quakers among them), lacking understanding of the total population situation, have wanted four children or more, and it appears that families of such size spell demographic disaster. Will it become necessary to use some kind of social coercion to avoid disaster? Can we not find more morally acceptable ways of solving the problem of numbers?

In the search for answers to such questions as these, it would be helpful to re-examine some of the beliefs and traditions of Friends in terms of their relevance for today.

Some Quaker Beliefs

The most basic belief of Friends is that every human being has the capacity to respond to the spirit of God, the "Light Within." It follows, therefore, that every human being is worthy of respect and reverence and that every human personality is sacred. Quaker concern for the quality of life of the individual and of society follows logically from these beliefs. The conviction of the universality of that of God in every man has caused Quakers historically to avoid following customs that discriminate against individuals, races, or nations. It explains Quaker involvement in prison reform and Quaker concern for the treatment of mental patients at a time when they were generally regarded as less than human. It explains Quaker involvement in the freeing of slaves and is at the center of the work of the American Friends Service Committee. It is the reason for the traditional attitudes of Friends against the taking of human life in war and in capital punishment. The deliberate destruction of a human being is considered a moral evil for two reasons: Killing destroys that of God in the victim; the one who kills violates his own divine potential, and this—perhaps more than the physical death of the victim—is the moral tragedy.

Emphasis on the importance of the Light Within has had ethical significance in Quaker history for another reason. The belief that each man can hear and respond to the leading of the spirit of God implies that revelation or the discovery of truth is not limited to the past or to any particular spokesman; rather it is a continuing process in which new revelations of truth place the earlier revelations in a deeper context. What was a right course of action yesterday may not be the right one today; and what seems right today may not be appropriate in tomorrow's situation.

Current ethical and religious standards are based primarily on tradition and habit. In Christian teachings the fetus had an absolute right to life. It was believed that what was right for the unborn child (life) was also best for the mother (moral integrity) and that both would coincide with what was good for the nation and for mankind (population maintenance and growth). The Biblical injunction "Be fruitful and multiply" was more than a blessing. Obedience to that precept was vital to the survival of the society of that day.

Does morality demand a different view today? Is our modern world different in such important and relevant ways from the world of the past that there are compelling reasons to question the traditional conclusions? What is the relevance to our ethical view of contraception and abortion, of the threat of overpopulation, the changed position of women, especially in the West, the development of medical knowledge, the prevalence of illegal abortions? If the new world is to a large degree new because of man's technological interference in the natural course of things, does this imply that man must also find a way of coping with the resulting problems?

In exploring these questions, we were reminded that Friends and others have tended to identify ethical standards with religious sanctions. But ethics is often relative or concerned with particular situations; and religious sanction, once thought of as derived from external authority, may be now as traditional and illogical as superstition. Even in older ways of thinking there is often inconsistency and contradiction. In the matter of abortion, the immediate concern for the welfare of individuals, the family, and society as a whole may conflict with what seems otherwise a desirable absolute standard.

Caught between distasteful alternatives and faced with the need to make a difficult choice, how do we decide which moral value should have priority?

Chapter 4

Man's Control
over Death

MAN'S CONQUEST of many of the causes of death, and his continuing discoveries of new ways to prolong life, pose religious and ethical questions as difficult to resolve as those concerned with the beginning of life.

Finding ways to save lives, to preserve and promote health, and to stave off death have been and continue to be causes that are universally approved. Far from encountering opposition, these goals have had wide support: from members of the public who want to live and to keep those they love alive as long as they can; from physicians whose traditional goal has been to save the lives of their patients; from scientists to whom research is a challenge; and from legislators who are sensitive to public interests and desires.

Increased Life Expectancy

The results are impressive. Death rates have been drastically reduced by advances in biomedical science and technology (improved sanitation and nutrition, developments in agriculture and in the storage and transportation of food, modern methods of insect control, sulfa drugs, vaccines, antibiotics, intravenous fluids, resuscitative apparatus). Millions of infants who would once have died now live to bear children of their own. Children suffering from severe physical disorders and from congenital diseases have been helped to survive. The death of women in childbirth is no longer common. The annual death toll from epidemics and disease (smallpox, cholera, tuberculosis, diphtheria, malaria, measles, yellow fever), once counted in the millions, is now negligible in Western nations and falling in others. Irrigation, flood control, agricultural advances, and improved transportation and communication have reduced the number of deaths from famine, flood, drought, and other catastrophes.

In the last one hundred years life expectancy has doubled —to seventy years or more in the industrialized nations and to fifty or more in most of the other countries; and it is continuing to increase. An ever-growing number of new drugs, skills, and devices is being used to control certain fatal diseases and to prolong the lives of the dying. Resuscitation applied quickly enough can bring the dead back to life. Machines are prolonging the lives of many with diseased kidneys by taking over the job of eliminating impurities from the blood. Machines are doing the work of breathing for paralyzed lungs. Hearts are being repaired with artificial valves and are being helped to function with implanted cardiac pacemakers. Now medical science is transplanting organs to replace malfunctioning kidneys, livers, and hearts. Hundreds of kidney transplants have already been performed, and in one year ninety-five human hearts were transplanted. In April of 1969 the first mechanical heart helped a dying man to live briefly until a human heart became available for transplantation.

Prolongation of Life in the Dying

The most recent medical advances and others now in progress—including further work on mechanical hearts—have focused attention on the special problems created by the ability to prolong life in the dying. Clergymen, doctors, lawyers, government leaders, and, increasingly, the general public are probing some of the basic ethical, medical, legal, and social questions implicit in this new power over life and death.

When and how should this power be used? Always, or under what circumstances? Should a life that has become hopeless and a burden to the individual and his family be artificially prolonged? Is the individual's life sacred when his brain has stopped functioning, when he can no longer relate to others? How do we balance concern for the preservation of life in the afflicted individual and concern for the quality of his life and that of his family and society?

The physician needs answers urgently, for he has the heaviest and most immediate responsibility. He has always had to make decisions about the patient who is threatened with death, but until recently he had relatively little power to influence the outcome. Now his decisions are affected by new knowledge and new tools that give him some control over the time of death and the nature of dying. In making these decisions, the physician is often torn between his obligation to preserve life and his obligation to relieve suffering and to allow the patient, if he must die, to die with comfort and dignity. Given a patient who in the doctor's best medical judgment has no chance of recovery, what should he do? To what lengths should he go to prolong the patient's life?

If the patient is hopelessly ill and in agonizing pain, should the physician try to keep him alive? Or should he

administer heavy doses of drugs to relieve the suffering, even though this may hasten death?

If the patient is unconscious for a very long time and is therefore unaware of pain but will never again be able to think and move and act, should the physician continue to struggle to keep him alive? For how long?

If a patient whose lungs have been permanently paralyzed by polio and whose brain has been irreparably damaged by lack of oxygen is being kept alive through a tracheotomy, artificial respiration, and intravenous feeding, should these procedures be continued indefinitely?

If a dying person is the potential donor of an organ for transplantation, the physician knows the urgency of performing the operation immediately after the death of the donor; at the same time his first responsibility is for the care of his patient. But when is the patient dead? Is he still alive if his heart beats and he breathes but his brain has stopped functioning?

If the life of the dying person might be prolonged by a transplanted or artificial organ, what should the physician advise? Such operations are becoming more and more successful; patients receiving kidneys from suitable closely related donors (parents or siblings) now have as much as a 75 per cent chance of surviving at least one year. Transplantation of the heart, a much newer procedure, is so far much more hazardous: At the end of the first year that the procedure was used, only five of the ninety-five recipients of hearts were still living. Thus, life is prolonged for an uncertain length of time, although some patients on chronic dialysis programs for kidney failure have lived as long as nine years, and some with kidney transplants have done almost as well. The question, however, remains: Is the extra life span and the degree of rehabilitation worth the discomfort, the psychological hazards, the long hospital stay, the enormous cost, and the tying up of a large part of a hospital staff when other patients need care?

With a shortage of transplantable organs, lifesaving machines, and other medical facilities, the physician also faces the painful task of deciding who shall be given a chance to live and who must be left to die. On what basis must he decide? Who is most likely to be rehabilitated? Who will contribute most? Who is needed most? Whether the potential and the quality of the life that would be saved is worth saving, balanced against other lives that might be saved? Or simply first come, first served?

Each case poses a separate problem, and the answer always involves making a value judgment about the quality of the patient's remaining life, as well as estimating its possible length. The judgment is never easy to make. The physician's decision about what to do or not to do for an apparently dying patient is necessarily tempered by the knowledge that he is not infallible, that he may be wrong in his diagnosis and his prognosis.

Ethical Implications of Medical Decisions

The ethical implications of the choices before him are also deeply troubling. If the motivation is compassion for the suffering, how does omission of therapy differ ethically from stopping artificial support once it has started, or from actively helping a patient to die? Is it an act of mercy or of murder to turn the respirator off or to stop the artificial feeding?

Theologians and lawyers, as well as physicians, have considered this dilemma. Perhaps the most famous pronouncement on it by a Christian church is that of Pope Pius XII. In 1957, in response to a question as to whether a doctor should stop artificial respiration in a dying patient, he replied that the doctor should use ordinary but not extraordinary means to prolong life. If extraordinary treatment (such as the use of a respirator) is stopped, the patient dies not from that act but from the underlying disease or injury.

But the physician knows that what is extraordinary treatment today may be ordinary treatment tomorrow.

A number of physicians believe that every effort must be made to prolong life, artificially if necessary, for reasons that seem to them convincing: Prolonging life buys time for the patient's natural recovery processes to act; miraculous and inexplicable recoveries have taken place in patients who had once been given up for dead; there is always the hope that a sudden new medical breakthrough may provide a more effective and longer-lasting treatment. A few physicians believe that withholding life-prolonging support, even in extreme cases, may encourage the progressive undermining of the principles that protect the sanctity of life.

In this last connection, Ralph B. Potter, Jr., of Harvard Divinity School, raises questions about the ethics of balancing the continuing effort to sustain life in a dying patient against social and economic considerations and the needs of others:

Once it is established that it is not always morally obligatory to support life with all the means at one's disposal, it is uncertain where the "balancing logic" will lead. Should support be withheld not only from the irreversibly comatose but also from those whose afflictions, though borne bravely, impose a severe load upon their society? Will those in the habit of balancing other values against life itself gradually seek greater benefits by expunging life where the gain seems large and the loss small?

A growing number of reputable and compassionate physicians disagree. They believe that the decision to extend treatment so far but no farther must take into account the interests of society and the wishes and condition of the patient and family. They agree with the religious approach that it may be God's will and an act of love to give up a life that no longer has meaning as a human person.

The physician is always aware of the suffering patient's family and the need to make his decision in consultation with them. To the family the patient continues to be a loved person; they may find it difficult to accept the fact that in his hopelessly unconscious state he is a mindless nonperson. If they continue to pay the tremendous cost of therapeutic measures, they may sacrifice the future development of other members of the family; if they do not continue to do everything possible, they may carry a heavy burden of guilt.

A New Definition of Death

A changed definition of death may in the near future provide guidance in reaching decisions in at least some of these cases. The medical definition of death, accepted by the law, is the cessation of heartbeat and respiration. But new medical knowledge raises questions about the adequacy of this definition. It is now known that different organs and tissues die at different rates, that it is possible to revive a heart after it has stopped beating and to keep both heart and lungs functioning by artificial means. Many medical scientists now believe that the definition of death should concern cessation of brain activity rather than heartbeat and respiration.*

It is crucial, for the doctor's protection, that the medical profession agree on a definition that is acceptable to the legal profession. Otherwise the physician might have to face civil liability or criminal action if a patient's family brings suit on grounds of failure to use every possible means to prolong life or if a vital organ has been removed before the patient is legally dead.

Euthanasia

A most difficult and highly controversial ethical question relates to euthanasia—the deliberate act of ending the life of a suffering person. The issues are well known.

---

* See Appendix VI for the new definition of death now being widely discussed in medical circles.

Opponents of euthanasia stress the sanctity of life and ask whether it is ever morally right to take the life of another human being, even if he begs to die. Might not the sufferer be only temporarily depressed and have a different outlook the following day or week or month? Might not the physician be wrong about the hopelessness of the case? If euthanasia were approved, would hard-pressed families facing economic ruin or the necessity of sacrificing the education of their children because of the patient's costly illness be encouraged to decide that the sufferer's life should be ended? What of the temptation to unscrupulous persons who stand to inherit under a patient's will? And finally, might a society in which life comes to be held cheap some day find reasons other than compassion for eliminating the old and unproductive or others whom the state considers a burden or a threat?

Speaking for euthanasia, Joseph Fletcher, the theologian, defends "our right to die," on the grounds that the quality of life or personality is far more important than mere physical existence, that severe pain and suffering may demoralize personality, destroy personal integrity, and thus negate the importance of life and its quality. He believes that compassion for the patient, the duty of the physician to relieve suffering as well as to heal, and even more his duty to the human personality that is being destroyed by unconsciousness or unbearable pain justify positive action to end life.

Frequently physicians decide in favor of their responsibility to relieve pain, and they administer heavy doses of drugs, knowing this may bring an earlier death. Or, unwilling to make such a decision, they sometimes leave drugs with the family, pointing out the consequences of large doses, with the knowledge that the family may decide it is right to end the patient's misery.

Under the law, which is based on the sanctity of human life, a deliberate act to end the life of another human being, whether it is performed by a doctor or anyone else, is illegal regardless of the intention. The legal status of an act of omission of therapy that results in the death of the patient is less certain; it is based not on the sanctity of life but on the relationship of the doctor to his patient. Perhaps for this reason no doctor has been convicted for causing death by omission of treatment for compassionate reasons.

Social Effects of Prolonged Life Span

The lengthening of the life span, as well as prolongation of life in the dying, has created difficult problems for the individual, the family, and society. These will become more and more acute as medical science continues to add years to our lives. The dimensions of future problems are foreshadowed by the conditions under which many older people in the United States live today.

Since most university, industrial, and government employees face compulsory retirement at the age of sixty-five, many people find that when they reach their sixty-fifth birthdays—no matter how able, mentally alert, and physically vigorous they are—their careers and their remunerative working lives are over. In 1967 more than one third of the 17,500,000 Americans who had reached retirement age were over seventy-five, and one million were eighty-five.

What are they doing with these postretirement years? A fortunate minority build second careers, take less demanding employment, turn to cherished avocations, or have inner resources that give life meaning. But the majority suddenly feel old and unwanted; their income is greatly reduced; they must change their style of living; they miss the daily contacts with working associates; they find their days empty or try to fill them with "busy work" that brings no satisfaction; their boredom and purposelessness grow as the endless hours drag on; their mental and physical health deteriorates. Nursing homes and the geriatric wards of mental hospitals are full of lonely, depressed men and women, confused, apathetic, dependent, senile, often unconscious, waiting to die.

To their children they often become a psychological as well as a financial burden. In these days of apartment living and working wives, it is not always possible or desirable for aging parents to live with married children, even if they wish to; their care in nursing homes is costly; younger people know their parents hate living in institutions and, in consequence, feel guilty and miserable for providing institutional care.

Society has tried to meet some of these problems. Public and private agencies have been creating opportunities for employment of the aging; they conduct classes in arts and crafts; promote social gatherings, lectures, "golden age" and "senior citizen" clubs, various recreational activities; build nursing homes and retirement centers; do research on the needs and problems of the old; offer preretirement advice on successful aging. But in spite of these efforts, most older people have not achieved a satisfactory quality of life; at sixty-five they still find they have little to look forward to.

And still the struggle to prolong life continues. Some day in the not-too-distant future it will probably be possible to replace worn-out hearts with artificial organs, and the manufacture of mechanical hearts may become one of our largest industries.

This preoccupation with extending life farther and farther raises questions that society must examine. Is prolonging life indefinitely a desirable end in itself? What are we prolonging it for?

When Adam and Eve ate of the fruit of the Tree of Knowledge, they lost their immortality. Do we really want it back?

Chapter 5

The Quality of Life

THE MEMBERS of the Working Party sought religious and moral answers to the questions of life and death discussed above, in terms of their effect on the quality of life that Friends desire for people everywhere.

The Good Life

We were aware that the definition of a satisfying life varies with differences in background, culture, and values, but also that all people share certain basic needs that must be met before any decent life is possible. In thinking through what we meant by "the quality of life," therefore, we took for granted satisfaction of these basic needs: adequate food, shelter, and clothing; physical and mental health; loving and being loved, belonging, and being able to function in one's society.

To Friends, a good life means much more. It means, in

addition, the opportunity to develop in mind, personality, and body to one's fullest potential. It means access to education and a healthy environment. It means the chance to grow up with dignity and self-respect in a family that encourages personal and social responsibility and helpfulness to others. It means a life in which man can make responsible use of his powers—physical, intellectual, creative, social, spiritual.

For a majority of people in the world, this quality of life seems an impossible dream. As more and more millions are added to our crowded earth and man continues his profligate use of limited resources, the prospect that the world's peoples may attain such a goal grows daily more remote. But it is in this direction that Friends wish to move.

How close we come to that goal depends on the attitudes and values instilled by millions of individual families, the decisions they make, the practices they follow. A major concern of Friends, therefore, has always been with family life, responsible parenthood, and the nurture of children.

Within the Family

It is in the family that the fortunate child of responsible parents finds the opportunity to develop the individuality that will make him a creative member of the larger society. It is in the family that he learns sensitivity to the feelings of others and understanding of their needs. It is in the family that he learns the meaning of personal responsibility, cooperation, and service. From the way his parents discharge their parental responsibilities and the way they treat others, he develops his own attitudes toward childrearing and society. His views on love and marriage and sex are strongly influenced by the relationship of his parents. If they have a satisfying relationship, he learns from them that a successful marriage depends on affection, respect, shared interests, and the ability to communicate; that at its best marriage is a union of two individuals who have learned to know and accept themselves and to understand and value each other and who find in their life together deepened awareness of the meaning of love, faithfulness, self-sacrifice, self-realization, and joy. The child learns that physical intimacy, important as it is, is only one aspect of a complex relationship, that the sexual act can be an act of love, a consummation that joins together in body two who are already close in spirit.

Clearly, parenthood imposes responsibilities too formidable to be entered into lightly. Thoughtful parents know that they must plan their families carefully if they are to have the kind of family life that will encourage the healthy development and nurture of their children. They want to take into account the resources in money, time, and personality they can bring to the task.

How many children will they be able to support adequately? What will it cost to feed, clothe, and educate each child, to keep him healthy, to prepare him for the vocation of his choosing? How much money must be set aside for things that add to the fullness of family life and therefore to the child's development into a responsible and responsive adult: for books and music, for exploration of the natural world, for mind- and soul-stretching experiences, for help to others, for important social causes? How much should be saved for unexpected emergencies? for the future?

How much time can husband and wife give to their children? It takes time to know and understand a child, to determine the limits that must be set on his behavior, to teach him to co-operate in the daily life and work of the family so that he may be prepared to co-operate with others in the larger society of neighborhood, school, and nation. It takes time to stimulate his personality to develop in its own way. It takes time to lead him toward self-discipline and self-reliance and to provide opportunities for privacy and solitude. And there must be time to laugh and play with him and to love him. Enlightened young people who are aware of the importance of limiting the size of their families often do not weigh carefully enough the wisdom of adequate spacing of births so that each of their two or three children has the time and attention he needs from a mother who is not exhausted from caring for little ones too close together in age.

Thoughtful couples also wish to consider their suitability for parenthood. Are they too young, too old, too impatient, too imprudent, too unstable, too self-engrossed, too involved in their careers for successful parenthood? Is their relationship so strained and unhappy that it might have an unhealthy emotional effect on children? Are there possible genetic defects that might be a threat to the normal development of a child?

Such considerations as these are at the core of responsible parenthood. Pope Paul VI discussed family planning in these words:

. . . it is for the parents to decide, with full knowledge of the matter, on the number of their children, taking into account their responsibilities toward God, themselves, the children they have already brought into the world, and the community to which they belong. . . .

It is in the context of a loving relationship between husband and wife and concern for the welfare of the total family that decisions should be made about contraception. In this same context, couples may feel that they must consider abortion when the burden of an unplanned-for child seems to threaten the quality of the family's life.

While not all good marriages produce children, careful planning and skilled counseling often result in helping couples who want and need children to experience the fulfillment of parenthood. Sometimes infertility can be corrected by medical advice and treatment. Artificial insemination is a possibility if the couple feels comfortable about this procedure. Couples who avoid parenthood because of knowledge of possible genetic defects may learn through genetic counseling that their fears are unwarranted or that science has discovered a way to prevent damage to their children. Or couples may find joy in adopting children already born who need their love.

Fortunately for the world, not all people want children. Some couples choose to substitute creativity for procreativity and produce "brain children" rather than those of flesh and blood. Responsible marriages that contribute both to the enrichment of the couple and to society often develop through such dedication. Some couples, because of a genetic heritage they fear, choose for mercy's sake to remain childless, and a small minority do so from a sense of social responsibility. In view of the population explosion, the wisdom of encouraging voluntary childlessness is being discussed increasingly as a service to the world. Where once people were urged to have as many children as possible for the good of society, today they are being urged to restrict reproduction for the same reason.

Couples who are incompatible do well to refrain from parenthood. Having a child in the hope that it will bring temperamentally unsuited people together has proved in most cases to lead to even greater unhappiness, for the child as well as for its parents. If either marriage partner finds his development dwarfed or threatened by the demands of the other, it is time for re-evaluation under spiritual guidance. Skilled counseling may help the couple to a better relationship.

Sometimes, however, divorce may be the only way out of a situation that seriously threatens the quality of family life. Such cases are common when two people rush into marriage because of premarital pregnancy; marry on the strength of physical attraction alone; have differences so great that they cannot be adjusted; fail to realize their unrealistic hope of changing or "reforming" each other; or through long association develop a "spiritual allergy" toward each other. In such cases people ought to be separated. Children should not be used as a reason for remaining together, for often an unhappy home is more harmful to the healthy emotional development of children than life with only one parent.

At its best, family life involves more than just parents and children. Many parents are long lived, and it is not uncommon to have living great-grandparents. Growing children have contacts with older family members whether they live in the same house or elsewhere. If the quality of family life fosters meaningful relationships, the continuity of life and love from generation to generation provides a sense of security and hope. The love, respect, and consideration parents show their own aging parents condition the young in similar attitudes toward their elders. Ideally, too, contacts with grandparents and great-grandparents through satisfying family relationships lead to compassionate understanding of the problems of growing old, to a sense of responsibility for the quality of life of old people in their last difficult years, and, finally, to acceptance of death as a necessary part of life.

Chapter 6

Some Answers
for Today

IN OUR Working Party discussions we considered many of
the obstacles to the attainment of a satisfying quality of life
within the family and in the larger society. We pondered
the issues described in preceding pages and, as expected, we
raised many more questions than we were able to answer.
But we arrived at an unexpected unity on the answers we did
reach. We present them for your consideration as the contribution of a small group of concerned individuals to current thinking on these issues. In doing so, we re-emphasize
the possible transiency of our present views. Time, developments now in progress, and factors yet unforeseen may, probably will, lead to new insights. The following "answers"
represent our considered judgment today.

Contraception and Control of Fertility

We believe that the population crisis is so threatening
to the quality of human life that for the sake of the indi-

vidual, the family, and society, we must bring population and resources into balance by learning to control our fertility. Toward this end, we believe that contraception is by far preferable to abortion. But we also believe that abortion, performed under proper conditions, is preferable to the birth of an unwanted child.

We believe that every child should be wanted by and born into a family that is able to feed, clothe, educate and, above all, love him; that the family is the basic unit of our society and that the married life of the parents should encompass sexual activity whether or not for purposes of procreation; that appropriate contraception, which spaces children and eliminates the fear of unwanted pregnancies, strengthens family ties and establishes a sense of responsible parenthood; that in view of the problem of overpopulation, every couple has a responsibility to society, as well as to their own family, not to overburden the world with more lives than it can sustain.

To help in achieving these purposes and discharging these responsibilities, we think that contraceptive information and services should be readily available. This means that every couple should have easy access to advice on family planning; to information on contraceptives and contraceptive methods; to whatever equipment and techniques are best suited to their particular situation and to their cultural and religious beliefs; and to inexpensive or free contraceptives and instruction in their use.

Opposition to easy access to contraceptives (as well as to a permissive approach to abortion) is often based on the belief that this would stimulate sexual immorality, that unmarried young people would be encouraged to have sexual relations when they might otherwise have refrained for fear of the consequences.

The facts indicate that fear of pregnancy, venereal disease, and detection has not been much of a deterrent to premarital sexual experience, at least in the United States and other

Western countries. A special study of Detroit marriages, involving interviews with couples and matching the date of first birth with the date of marriage, showed that 54 per cent of a sample of girls marrying under age eighteen and 26 per cent of girls aged eighteen to nineteen were pregnant at the time of marriage. Three fourths of premarital conceptions under age twenty are resolved by marriage. In England, the general figure for pregnancy at the time of marriage, for girls under eighteen, is a little over 50 per cent; in Scotland, 60 per cent. It is also known that thousands of older teen-age girls in Detroit ask their doctors for abortions each year; presumably many secure them. It seems reasonable to conclude that sexual intercourse is very common among older teenagers. Over 90 per cent of university students in the same area denied that freer access to contraceptives (and to abortion) would lead them to increase their sexual activity.

We believe that, faced with the moral necessity to choose among difficult alternatives, offering freer access to contraceptives represents a better choice than illegal abortion or the birth of an unwanted child. And the benefits to both individuals and society seem to us to outweigh by far any possible risk of encouraging promiscuous relationships. These benefits include helping the most vulnerable groups in the population—the poor, the young, and the unmarried—to control their fertility; reducing illegitimacy; reducing the number of school dropouts, interrupted vocations, hasty marriages, divorces, and broken homes; preventing the birth of possibly damaged, deprived, and unwanted children; relieving population pressures.

Moreover, we believe that it is wrong as well as ineffective to use either law or the fear of consequences to enforce moral standards; that punishing a woman with an unwanted pregnancy and condemning a child to a blighted life to buttress morality are both socially irresponsible and morally indefensible.

We suggest that it is the responsibility of the family and

the school to develop healthy attitudes toward sexual behavior. Parents and teachers are becoming increasingly aware
that setting up a standard of chastity, supported only by fear
of the physical and social consequences of premarital sexual
intercourse, is not an effective way to advise young people.
The young know that some of the consequences can be
avoided, and they reject prohibitions and old definitions of
sexual morality. A definition that we believe expresses values
acceptable to youth was stated by Evelyn M. Duvall and
Reuben Hill:

A man is moral to the extent that he sincerely cherishes his mate
and seeks her welfare in his conduct with her. He uses the sex act
as a way of expressing the deepest feeling and the highest values
man and woman have for each other.

A woman is moral as she values her man as an end in himself,
rather than as a means for the furtherance of her own personal
goals alone.

They both behave morally as they find with each other selfless
devotion as well as self-gratification, lasting loyalty as well as mo-
mentary pleasure, and commitment to their larger responsibilities
as well as their satisfaction with each other.*

The demands of human sexuality are great, and the desire
for physical satisfaction can be almost overpowering. Often
young people turn to masturbation for relief. Once thought
physically and psychologically harmful, this is now considered
by psychiatrists to be a normal, healthy outlet that does not
interfere with later marital adjustment.

Sex education is essential to understanding sex drives and
to dealing with them responsibly. But it is the example of
the loving relationship of parents and the atmosphere of
trust and affection they create in the home that have the
most profound effect on the attitudes of their children toward
sexual responsibility. Ideally, young people exposed to en-
during values in personal relationships will come to think of

* From *Being Married* by E. M. Duvall and R. Hill. Copyright ©, 1960,
by D. C. Heath and Co., Boston Mass.

To relieve quote abortion

the sex act as the final communication of love between people who have already learned to communicate in other ways and have already committed themselves to each other.

In support of our position on birth control, and as a means toward achieving the highest possible quality of life for individuals, their families, and the world community, we urge:

1. Sex education in the home, beginning at an early age, bolstered by the kind of parental relationships and example described above.
2. Sex education in both public and private schools, beginning when children enter school, designed to develop understanding of the meaning of sex, the importance of sexual responsibility, the need for family planning, and the responsibilities of parenthood.
3. Training to equip teachers to teach, at appropriate age levels, about human biology and reproduction, sexuality, marriage and family living, and family planning and its relevance to world population problems.
4. The provision of publicly supported family planning services for the general public, in addition to freely available supplies through public, private, and commercial channels.

Voluntary Versus Involuntary Control of Family Size

We believe that responsible parenthood demands consideration not only of the number of children individual parents want but also of the effect of that number on society as a whole.

As the world becomes ever more crowded, an average of more than two children per family will inevitably lead to a diminished quality of life for all. Garrett Hardin writes of the need for "mutual coercion mutually agreed upon." He states:

The only way we can preserve and nurture other more precious freedoms is by relinquishing the freedom to breed, and that very soon. "Freedom is the recognition of necessity"—and it is the role of education to reveal to all the necessity of abandoning the freedom to breed.*

Other writers have suggested ways of restructuring society to produce the incentives necessary to limit population. These suggestions range from intensified educational programs and bonuses or tax benefits for small families, to establishing creative jobs for women outside the home, or even to such extreme measures as compulsory surgical sterilization.

Some of these proposals invite discriminatory attempts at population limitation by one group upon another. If they were put into effect, minority groups might well question the motivation behind them, however good and well-intentioned it might be. Attempts at compulsion toward large family size have been futile; there is no reason to believe that similar attempts toward small family size would be any more successful. And the feeling and conflict engendered by any compulsory program might be so bitter and so fraught with undesirable social and political consequences as to corrode the quality of life we wish to attain.

We believe that the necessary limitation of family size should be and can be achieved voluntarily by far more attention to the adequate availability of contraceptives, by the legalization of abortion, and by educational programs to motivate people to practice family planning. For the good of all, we should educate ourselves and others to the necessity of restricting family size as a prerequisite for a life of quality for our children's children and for the generations to follow.

There is cause for hope in the fact that in recent years Japan, Hungary, and Rumania, where abortion has been available

* "The Tragedy of the Commons," *Science*, 162 (December 1968), 1243–1248. Copyright 1968 by the American Association for the Advancement of Science.

on request, managed to achieve fertility rates which, if maintained, would lead to stabilization of the population. For the
United States, the estimated number of unwanted children and
the number of births in excess of those necessary to maintain a
stationary population are so nearly similar as to indicate that
the population could be stabilized if only children who are
wanted were born.* It seems, therefore, that unless fertility
rates change, the provision of adequate total health care, including contraception and access to abortion without legal
restriction, might go a long way toward reducing the number
of unwanted births and the threat of overpopulation in our
country.

Abortion

We believe that no woman should be forced to bear an
unwanted child. A woman should be able to have an abortion legally if she has decided that this is the only solution
she can accept and if the physician agrees that it is in the
best interests of mother and child. She should be encouraged to seek the best social and spiritual counseling available before reaching a decision; and the physician, for his
own support, should have the opportunity to confer with
colleagues of his choosing if he feels the need for such
consultation.

Believing that abortion should be subject to the same
regulations and safeguards as those governing other medical and surgical procedures, we urge the repeal of all laws
limiting either the circumstances under which a woman may
have an abortion or the physician's freedom to use his best
professional judgment in performing it.

We believe that no physician should be forced to perform an abortion if this violates his conscience; but, if this

* See Appendix II.

is so, he has an obligation to refer his patient to another physician willing to serve her.

We were drawn to these conclusions by facts and considerations that bear repetition.

The need for abortions may be greatly reduced when contraceptives that are as acceptable, effective, and safe as possible become readily available. But until that time, it can be assumed from the evidence that women will continue to have abortions. No prohibitions or penalties anywhere in the world have succeeded in stopping them. Instead, restrictive laws have made them more difficult to obtain, more dangerous, and more degrading.

Current laws in the United States are discriminatory, since the rich find it possible to secure abortions unobtainable by the poor. They promote criminal activity and disrespect for law. They are an invasion of human rights: the right of a child to be wanted and loved, the right of a woman to decide whether and when she will have children. And, by interfering with the right of families to limit the number of their children, present laws contribute to population pressures.

While we found all of the above considerations persuasive and important, the most decisive factors in reaching our conclusions have been our concern that the individual, the family, and society achieve the highest possible quality of life and our conviction that this is unlikely for mentally and physically damaged or unwanted children, for their parents, and for an overpopulated world.

On religious, moral, and humanitarian grounds, therefore, we arrived at the view that it is far better to end an unwanted pregnancy than to encourage the evils resulting from forced pregnancy and childbirth. At the center of our position is a profound respect and reverence for human life, not only that of the potential human being who should never have been conceived, but of the parents, the other children, and the community of man.

The repeal of abortion laws seems to us to be a step in the right direction, but much more is needed:

1. Positive programs to do away with the necessity for abortions, as summarized on page 62.
2. A program of medically sound and easily available abortion services at low cost to protect women against the health problems resulting from recourse to back-street abortionists.
3. Abortion services as part of accepted medical care, paid for by public funds for those who depend on public funds for such care.
4. Availability of counseling and social services to women requesting abortion with a view to (a) helping them examine the alternatives to abortion, (b) exploring with them sources of aid—medical, financial, adoptive—to make possible carrying the baby to term and rearing it decently, (c) putting them in touch with social services equipped to deal with such other problems as employment and housing, and (d) providing contraceptive advice and education as protection against future unwanted pregnancies. It is society's responsibility to provide such counseling services where they are not now available.

In pursuing these approaches, we must not lose sight of the need to work toward larger goals—raising educational levels and standards of living—important to the quality of life both as ends in themselves and as necessary means of motivating people to control their fertility.

Genetic Counseling

We believe that married couples should have the benefit of the best medical and genetic counseling obtainable when genetic or congenital difficulties are anticipated in their children.

Many societies have recognized the desirability of discouraging certain types of matings: between parent and child, between siblings, or between first cousins, because such matings may result in an increased number of genetic abnormalities.

Some diseases or defects that are hereditary can be predicted to occur with a given frequency in a given family. Such predictions can be made for a limited number of diseases with varying degrees of reliability. Medical knowledge of genetics now permits the physician to advise couples who are carriers of dominant genetic or chromosomal defects of the risk to their potential offspring if they should decide to marry or to have children. Advising couples who are carriers of recessive gene defects is much more difficult since it may be impossible to know whether both parents are carriers until a defective child has been born. The possibility of detecting such carriers in both parents is increasing yearly as a result of biological research. In some cases, by prenatal diagnosis it is becoming possible to test for the presence of certain defects between the twelfth and twentieth weeks and end the pregnancy if the child is defective.

We believe genetic counseling should take into account the degree of risk involved, the seriousness of the possible defect, the parents' willingness to risk having a defective child in the hope of having a healthy one, the possibility that a child with such a defect might be helped by medical or surgical procedures to lead a comparatively normal life, and the possible result of the defect on the life of the child, on other members of the family, and on society.

On the basis of such considerations, prospective parents would be better equipped to decide whether or not to have children or, if conception has taken place, whether to seek an abortion.*

* Sources of genetic counseling are listed in an *International Directory of Genetic Services,* May 1968, published by the National Foundation—March of Dimes, 800 Second Avenue, New York, N. Y., 10017.

For the mentally retarded, we encourage genetic counseling and the availability of both abortion and sterilization on request of the guardian.

Although the mentally ill or retarded may well have normal children, inability to care for them properly may be the basis for the guardian's decision for abortion.

Medical science is now able to develop the capacity for parenthood in many cases once considered subjects for sterilization. Accordingly, increasing emphasis is being placed on contraceptives that control fertility over long periods but do not cause permanent infertility.

We are opposed to compulsory abortion and to compulsory sterilization and believe that such laws should be repealed.*

In cases of severe mental retardation where voluntary sterilization is refused, it may be necessary to institutionalize the afflicted persons in order to protect them and society.

Genetic Manipulation

"Positive" or "progressive" eugenics or direct genetic manipulation to improve the breeding of men seems to us to be socially and morally undesirable as well as scientifically impractical.

Some geneticists point out that new discoveries may make it possible to control hereditary diseases like hemophilia; wipe out diabetes and other diseases; eliminate birth defects related to genetic components; provide healthy new genes for mental defectives. Successful experiments on bacteria and other lower organisms indicate that eventually it may also be possible to alter the direction of human evolution. Among the future possibilities described by geneticists are the ability to preselect sex; to alter genetic traits; to program cells by

---

* In 1966, laws supporting these procedures were still on the books in twenty-seven states.

injecting new genetic materials; to improve the physical and mental characteristics of man; to remake defective children; to produce identical copies of people with superior characteristics.

We do not believe that it is wise to support a program of genetic manipulation in humans.

First, it is impossible to know what traits would be desirable in human beings who will live in the future and what traits should therefore be perpetuated. Genetic diversity is one of the strengths of mankind. Such diversity is needed to enable man to adapt to his social and physical environment; it is much more likely to develop men of high quality and adaptability than narrowing the gene pool.

Secondly, it takes thousands of generations of regimented reproduction to remove even the worst of genetic defects by breeding alone, because most of them are recessive and are not yet detectable in the apparently normal carrier.

Thirdly, even if the undesirable genes could be detected and eliminated, there might be the risk of losing good traits in the process.

And finally, the environment for people with specific genetically determined defects is being modified much more rapidly than compulsory breeding could modify the incidence of the defect. Thus the defects themselves are in essence made less serious.

The abuse of eugenics in the Nazi experiments points up some of the dangers of human manipulation to serve eugenic purposes. We believe that legal barriers to private and voluntary eugenics, such as artificial insemination, as well as to birth control and abortion, should be removed, and that some degree of preventive genetic counseling may be justified and helpful. But we are opposed to efforts to improve the human race by compulsory selected mating or by other compulsory methods; such efforts cannot be sanctioned or carried out in a society that respects the rights of individuals. We believe that society must examine the implications of the new science of genetic engineering and set limits on its application lest the ability to direct human evolution produce social and moral consequences disastrous to the future of man.

Prolongation of Life in the Dying

In arriving at answers to some of the questions relating to "death control" in Chapter 4, we took into account considerations of morality, compassion, and concern for the quality of life of all who are affected.

We believe human life is a gift that is meaningful only as long as the receiver is able to function as a person. The quality of the potential life left to the dying person must be a consideration constantly before concerned physicians and society to help guide their actions in specific cases.

We approve withholding therapy or withdrawing the supportive therapy that is keeping an unconscious person alive if, by evidence of brain death or such other evidence as the medical profession deems valid, it is the best judgment of the medical profession that the patient's brain is irreparably damaged and he will never recover consciousness.

The same considerations seem to us to relate also to the hopelessly unconscious patient who is being considered as the source for transplantation of an essential organ.

We believe it is important for the medical profession to arrive at a scientifically acceptable definition of unequivocal death of the brain to help physicians decide whether or not to continue efforts for patients who are already dead by this definition but whose hearts and lungs may be kept functioning indefinitely. Such a definition would protect the patient against forced continuance of a meaningless existence or against possibly premature organ removal; the physician against accusations of medical, moral, or legal misconduct; the family against the burden of long, fruitless, and emotionally exhausting medical care; and society against the cost of maintaining unproductive medical services.

We believe that society and the law should grant some discretion to the conscientious physician who prescribes narcotics for a dying patient in great pain.

Though death may result from this frequently carried out and compassionate act, the physician's primary intent is not to end life but to relieve suffering. We believe that the law and society should recognize explicitly that this is so, as they now recognize it implicitly.

We are not prepared to take an intelligent position on euthanasia, an act committed with the deliberate purpose of ending the life of a suffering person. This subject opens many problems and requires more careful consideration and much more searching study than our Working Party was prepared to give to it. We are aware that hopelessly ill people in pain and unwanted, destitute old people sometimes ask physicians to help them die. We are aware, too, of the possible dangers and abuses of euthanasia as a socially and legally acceptable solution. The problem needs to be considered by medical scholars, teachers, and students with a view to helping young doctors confront such pleas with insight, compassion, and intelligence. It calls for wise and thoughtful consideration by religious, legal, and social thinkers and by society at large. We suggest that the subject deserves special study and examination commensurate with its seriousness and complexity.

Death in Perspective

A searching look into the general attitude toward death may help to explain the current scientific preoccupation with finding new ways to keep people alive.

Pascal wrote: "Since men have not succeeded in eliminating death, they have decided not to think of it." It is strange but true that although the inevitability of eventual death is a fact that cannot be changed, many people refuse to think of it or become obsessed with fear of it.

We believe that death should be viewed in proper perspective, as a natural part of the process of life. We believe in its necessity and goodness, as well as in its inevitability.

Death, we know, is necessary to evolution. While some asexual single cells may be immortal, the price of their immortality is their sameness. Each separates into two others like itself, which in turn separate in similar fashion; over and over again each produces identical cells. The birth and death of the individual came with sexual reproduction. It made possible the mixture of different strains and heredities, the rise of new combinations, the changes and variations essential to the evolution of higher forms of life. New mutants would never have evolved into new forms to replace the old if the old forms had not disappeared. If man never died, the world would be cluttered up with the old. New generations could not develop, and evolution would stop.

Death is good when it comes as a blessing to end suffering or when, after a full and fruitful life, the senses fail and the will to live is gone. Death is good because it enables those who have already made their contributions to make room for the young and their contributions.

Perhaps a healthy perspective on death would lead us to devote our resources to making our lives better rather than longer. Perhaps such perspective would help us to think of immortality not as an unending personal life but in terms of our contributions to the continuity of culture, the memories we leave behind, and the heritage of thought and values we pass on to future generations.

It is for those future generations, as well as for ourselves, that we began the search for answers to help us face with wisdom, compassion, and moral responsibility the difficult issues of life and death.

Epilogue

Choosing Priorities

BEYOND the questions we have explored in this report are others of a broader nature, questions that we cannot attempt to answer now. These concern the choice of priorities.

The quality of our lives is inextricably bound to the choices we make, the priorities we set for the use of our own and society's resources. Such choices are especially painful and difficult when they relate directly to life and death. And many of the choices we are forced to make do determine who shall live and who shall die.

We establish priorities for ourselves and others all the time. We set them when we decide that abortion is all right because the potential life is not so valuable as the quality of life of the family and society. Relief workers set priorities whenever they undertake food programs in famine areas. They have only a limited amount of food to distribute. Who is to be fed? babies or school children? working men or pregnant women? the old and the sick or the young and the strong? Usually decisions have been governed by compassion for the weak.

Public health officials and physicians, given limited budgets, are continually called upon to make similarly hard decisions. Should they save congenitally defective babies, expand family planning services, or invest in a health program for school children? Which diseases should be given highest priority? Which groups should get chest X-rays and vaccinations?

It is estimated that seven thousand people die annually in the United States because their kidneys no longer function properly, individuals whose lives could be prolonged by periodic dialysis or transplanted kidneys. With limited numbers of donors and centers for transplantation, and with too few dialysis centers to serve more than a fraction of the afflicted, which lives should be saved? Which of the many victims of untreatable heart disease (estimated at eighty thousand annually) should get a heart transplant? If mechanical hearts, which may be perfected during the lifetime of many of us, become widely available, what choices will society then be called upon to make? Should an artificial heart be implanted in everyone who needs and wants one, on request of the physician? Or should only those who can be useful and productive again be helped to continue to live? Physicians faced with the need to make these difficult life-and-death choices should have, and in many cases already do have, the guidance of a panel of advisers.

The cost of life-prolonging medical advances presents other difficult choices. Resources for medical needs and medical research are not unlimited. A single heart transplant costs $20,000 to $50,000; a kidney transplant approximately $10,000. Thirty million dollars will buy the artificial kidney units needed to prolong the lives of victims of kidney failure. The government has stepped up its efforts to perfect an artificial heart, for which many more millions will be needed. Each of these expenditures can be justified. But society has a right to ask—and scientists have an obligation to answer—such questions as, What are the alternatives? What are some of the other uses to which these same funds might be put? By devoting such a large share of limited medical personnel, funds, hospital and research facilities to experiments and procedures that are keeping a relatively small number of people alive at great expense for a while longer, are we withholding these resources from many other lives whose quality might be greatly enhanced if different choices were made? Is the choice between research on an artificial heart for the old and preventing rheumatic heart disease in the young? between dialysis units and neighborhood health centers? How many individuals could be rehabilitated with glasses, hearing aids, or dental care for the cost of one heart transplant or one kidney unit?

In making choices we must remember that medical advances that cost millions of dollars in their research and experimental stages have resulted in making life possible or better for countless individuals, and that while the cost of services to the earliest beneficiaries of these advances was sometimes high, it was greatly reduced as techniques were perfected and adequate supplies became available.

The need for medical research and experimentation is clear. But here, too, we have choices to make. A substantial portion of medical research funds and facilities in recent years has been invested in efforts to prolong life in the aging or dying and to seek cures for specific diseases, mainly in the elderly. The value of every such program can be documented in human terms. But the problem remains: How do we allocate medical research resources between the needs of the aging and those of younger persons so that the quality of life may be enhanced for all?

In this connection we are confronted by a number of profound social and moral considerations. Is it *desirable* to keep increasing the life span of the general population? to what limit? If we could make it possible for people to live to be well over one hundred, *should* we? Would the added years be fulfilling and productive for the individual, his family, and society? Or would we simply be adding to the unhappiness of an ever-increasing number of people, compounding the problems of an already overburdened society, and aggravating the population crisis? Should additional millions be spent on helping the elderly to live longer, or should the money be spent on improving the quality of the life span we have already achieved?

Our public policies with respect to medical care often show evidence of ambivalence because we have not thought through our priorities in terms of our resources. For example, the government is spending large sums of money to provide medical care for those aged sixty-five and over; yet certain government-financed health agencies, lacking resources to provide prosthetic aids to all the needy, are having to refuse the requests of the aged in order to give priority to younger people. What benefit to the aging are added years if they cannot be helped to see and hear and eat? If as a society we are moving toward the concept of medical care as a right, how much medical care do we mean? Should this include not only artificial teeth and glasses but, some day, an artificial heart? Or should an age limit, similar to the age of forced retirement, be set for recipients of hearts—none available for anyone over sixty-five?

The many choices before us go far beyond setting priorities within the field of medicine. They involve priorities in allocating public and social resources among all of the many needs that must be met, domestic and foreign. Appropriations by Congress over the calendar year 1968 indicate the priorities set by our government. Of the total appropriations of more than $156 billion, 66 per cent was for military and defense-related purposes, and 15 per cent for human needs at home. These are some of the figures:*

---

* Based on a report in *Washington Newsletter,* Friends Committee on National Legislation, December 1968.

PURPOSE	APPROPRIATION (IN BILLIONS)
Military activities (exclusive of payments to veterans and other costs of past wars)	$80.7
Welfare	8.4
Health (including $2.6 billion for public health and $391 million for air and water pollution)	7.9
Agriculture and other natural resources	7.6
Education	5.1
Space exploration	3.9
Housing	2.1
Economic aid to the developing world	2.0

Does this represent the informed choices of society? What would the billions spent in the last few years on war have bought in slum improvement, education, housing, public health, nutrition?

Some of the choices made in the past have led to the poisoning of the environment in the United States and the world. While we have been spending enormous sums to cure illness, we have been creating new threats to health and life. Technological advances, industrialization, a rapidly increasing population, and urbanization have led to practices that are polluting the air and water, eroding and poisoning the soil, destroying forests and wildlife, contaminating the earth with wastes and pesticides and noxious fumes. Each year in the United States alone 142 million tons of smoke and poisonous fumes are dumped into the atmosphere.

The United States has set up legislation to prepare standards for the control of environmental pollution; and in December 1968 fifty-four countries introduced a resolution in the United Nations General Assembly calling for a 1972 international conference on pollution and human environment. In speaking to this resolution, the Swedish ambassador emphasized the seriousness of the problem resulting from man's technological advances:

Even if we avoid the risk of blowing up the planet, we may—by changing its face—unwittingly be parties to the same fatal outcome.

Protecting the human environment to prevent such an outcome would make cost—billions of dollars presumably— another factor in the choices we must make. During the 1968 calendar year Congress appropriated $391 million for such environmental protection. The cost of the first stage of the antiballistic-missile system is conservatively estimated at $7 billion. Do we want a healthy environment, or more military hardware?

Moral responsibility also places upon us the need to consider the effect of our actions on the quality of life of the rest of the world. Many of the world's resources other than food are in short supply. Among them are irreplaceable substances such as metals and oil. Yet the United States, with 6 per cent of the world's population, accounts for half the yearly consumption of these substances. What would happen if the peoples of the underdeveloped world succeeded in raising their standard of living to equal ours and plundered the earth to the same extent?

Concern over the poverty of most of the world has led to the suggestion that the problem be met by dividing the world's goods and distributing them equally. The thought, motivated by good will, may appeal to our humanitarian instincts, but even if such distribution could be managed, do we want to raise the quality of life of the poorer peoples by lowering appreciably the quality of other lives? If the total output of the world were to be divided equally among the people living in 1968, the average per capita income would be less than $500 a year. This compares with an average per capita income in the United States in 1968 of almost $2,900, and in Europe of more than $1,000. Thus, redistributing the world's income without finding ways to increase it and to limit population would simply result in universal poverty and the steady erosion of the quality of life.

We believe that the magnitude of the problem demands continuing comprehensive studies to determine:

1. What the resources of the world are and can be in terms of food and other necessary and distributable goods.
2. How many people these resources can support adequately.
3. What must be done to relate resources to population in ways designed to move in the direction of improving the quality of life for all.

Hopefully, such studies should also present the alternatives before the world. It would then be possible to make intelligent choices in adjusting national and international priorities for the allocation of public funds.

This is a task that calls for an international effort of vast scope. Individual agencies within the United Nations, such as the Food and Agricultural Organization and the World Health Organization, have been at work for years on certain vital aspects of the proposed studies. The United Nations investigation into pollution and the human environment soon to be undertaken would form another important part of the whole. We suggest the need for a much more comprehensive and concentrated effort than has yet been planned, conducted by a continuing study group drawn from all the relevant disciplines and made up of the most competent social thinkers, humanitarians, and scientists the world can offer.

The series of actions that are finally taken, and the quality of continuously evolving public policy, will depend on the extent to which citizens understand the issues and the choices before them and how they view their responsibilities to themselves, to their families, and to the world and its future. We stress society's obligation to be informed, to question, to analyze the facts, to evaluate, and to decide public policy after carefully weighing alternatives.

The quality of future human life, perhaps even the continued existence of man, depends on the priorities society chooses now and in the years immediately ahead. Too often in the past priorities have been determined and public funds have been allocated without careful weighing of alternatives. Sometimes decisions have been made because of pressure by special interests, because of the drama and challenge of scientific experimentation, for reasons of political expediency, national prestige, or military security, and sometimes simply because no one has had the courage to protest.

When the atomic bomb was developed and dropped on Hiroshima, the public was not informed in advance, for reasons of wartime secrecy, and had no opportunity to consider alternatives. Equally portentous choices face us now. Scientific advances and their impact on human life make it urgently necessary to choose our priorities wisely and responsibly.

Man in his relatively short span on earth has developed miraculous powers for good and for ill. Through his science he can influence the course of his own evolution. His science has made it possible for him to change the conditions of his daily life on earth, to alter his environment, to improve his health and prolong his life—and at the same time to threaten himself with extinction by nuclear holocaust, by overpopulation, and by poisoning his environment. Through the practical application of science in the industrial revolution, the cybernetic revolution with its development of automation, and the revolution brought about by nuclear energy, man has made it possible—if he will—to free himself from want. Yet he has not done so. Nor has he developed the moral and spiritual powers needed to cope with the social problems and responsibilities resulting from his scientific achievements.

The journey to the moon was hailed with wonder and rejoicing by a proud nation. The communications media were full of tributes to the magnitude of this achievement and the courage of the astronauts. But some also questioned the moral priorities that allowed us to spend billions to go to the moon when we have poverty and hunger on earth. An essay in *Time* magazine offered this perspective:

The triumph of Apollo 8 cannot erase the irony that it is easier for man to go to the moon than to wipe out a ghetto, easier for him to travel through space than to clean up his own polluted atmosphere, easier for him to establish cooperation in a vast technological enterprise than to establish brotherhood on a city block.*

Perhaps man's failure to solve some of the world's most compelling problems is not so much the result of inability as of lack of perspective or of motivation and determination. He has proved that he can do almost anything he sets out to do. But he has not always asked himself what he should do and why.

It is to these moral questions that Quakers and others seek answers as they face in their own lives and in their work the issues of life and death presented in this report.

* "Of Revolution and the Moon," *Time*, January 3, 1969, p. 17. Courtesy TIME; Copyright, Time Inc., 1969.

Appendix I

Population Data

The following figures and table indicate the major quantitative aspects of the population problem.

FIGURE 1 *

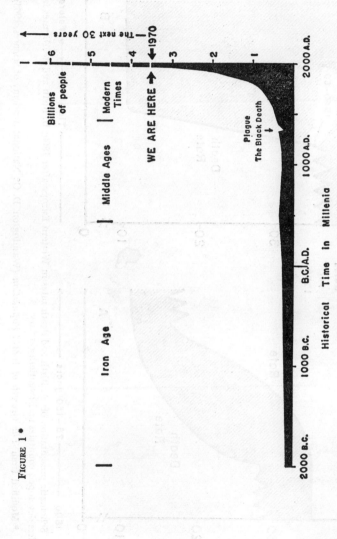

Historical Time in Millenia

Population growth over the past 4,000 years

* Modified from chart originally printed in *Population Bulletin* (Washington, D. C.: Population Reference Bureau).

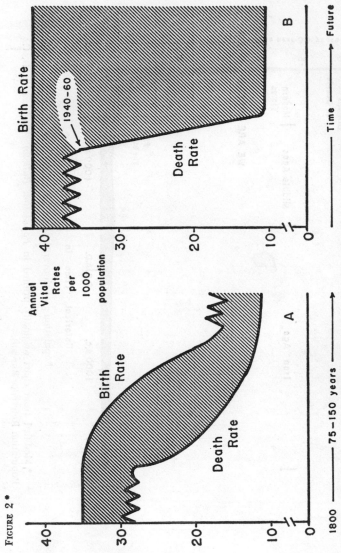

FIGURE 2 *

Schematic presentation of: A. Birth and death rates in Western Europe after 1800; B. Birth and death rates in less developed countries mid-twentieth century

* Modified from *The Growth of World Population* (Washington, D. C.: National Academy of Sciences, 1963).

TABLE 1   POPULATION STATISTICS FOR SELECTED COUNTRIES*

Country	Current Rate of Population Growth** (Per Cent)	Number of Years to Double Population	Birth Rate per 1,000 Population	Death Rate per 1,000 Population	Population under Fifteen Years (Per Cent)	Population Illiterate† Fifteen Years and over (Per Cent)
World	1.9	37	34	15	37	39
Costa Rica	3.8	18	45	7	38	10–20
Philippines	3.5	20	50	10–15	47	25–30
Honduras	3.4	21	49	17	51	50–60
Mexico	3.4	21	43	9	46	30–35
Pakistan	3.3	21	52	19	45	75–85
Peru	3.1	23	42	11	45	35–40
Kenya	3.0	23	50	20	46	70–75
UAR	2.9	24	43	15	43	75–80
Brazil	2.8	25	38	10	43	30–35
India	2.5	28	43	18	41	70–75
Turkey	2.5	28	46	18	44	60–65
Nigeria	2.5	28	50	25	43	80–88
Indonesia	2.4	29	43	21	42	55–60
Ivory Coast	2.3	31	56	33	43	85–92
Canada	2.0	35	18	7.3	33	0–3
New Zealand	1.9	37	22.4	8.4	33	0–1
Japan	1.1	63	19	6.8	25	0–2
USSR	1.0	70	18	8	32	0–2
United States	1.0	70	17.4	9.6	30	0–3
France	1.0	70	16.9	10.9	25	0–3
Poland	0.8	88	16.3	7.7	30	0–5
Sweden	0.8	88	15.4	10.1	21	0–1
Italy	0.7	100	18.1	9.7	24	5–10
United Kingdom	0.6	117	17.5	11.2	23	0–1
Hungary	0.3	233	14.6	10.7	23	0–5
Belgium	0.1	700	15.2	12.2	24	0–3

Source: World Population Data Sheet (April 1969), Population Reference Bureau, Washington, D. C. Figures for Population Illiterate Fifteen Years and Over from World Population Data Sheet (March 1968).

* See Appendix II for details concerning the calculation of birth, death, fertility, and growth rates.

** These rates include modifications by immigration and emigration.

† Literacy is defined as ability both to read and to write. The rates are affected by variations in the criteria used for judging literacy as well as by completeness of information.

Appendix II

Effect on Population Growth of Birth, Death, and Fertility Rates

DEATH RATES represent the number of deaths per thousand in the total population per year. These rates provide only a rough means of making comparisons between one country and another; they do not necessarily reflect the quality of the country's health services. Where there is a higher proportion of old people in a population, the death rate is naturally higher; a high proportion of young people produces a lower rate. For example, in Costa Rica, where infant and child mortality recently declined sharply and the proportion of young people is high, the death rate of 7 per thousand is lower than the 9.6 of the United States.

Birth rates represent the number of births per thousand in the total population per year. These rates are also influenced by the age structure of the population. The birth rate, however, is a less valid factor for comparison between countries than the fertility rate, which is a better index of reproductive performance.

Fertility rates represent the number of children born per

year to one thousand women of reproductive age (fifteen–forty-four inclusive). Data on fertility rates are not available for all countries and so are not included in Appendix I.

Population growth rates represent the per cent increase in population for one year. If there were no migration, the rate of population growth would be calculated by subtracting the death rate from the birth rate and converting the resulting figure to per cent by moving the decimal point. Kenya, for example, had a birth rate of 50 and a death rate of 20. The net gain is 30 per thousand, or 3 per cent. Canada is reported as growing at 2 per cent per year, yet the rate of natural increase (births minus deaths) is only 1.07 per cent.

Population grows like money in the bank at compound interest. A rough calculation can be made by dividing 70 by the percentage of yearly increase. Thus Canada, at 2 per cent per year, will double her population in thirty-five years. To illustrate the explosive nature of the current increases: In early historic times, the population doubled at the rate of about once in every two thousand years; in the one hundred years between 1850 and 1950, it doubled again. It is now doubling every thirty-five years. The scope of the population problem is further illustrated by the growth in numbers: The total world population in 1750, representing growth from prehistoric times to the middle of the eighteenth century, was only 750 million persons; if the world's current rate of growth continues, we would add more than 750 million in a single decade.

In 1936, a depression year, the birth rate in the United States was 18.4, and the fertility rate was 75.8. In 1968, a year characterized by prosperity and a war, the birth rate was *lower*, 17.4, but the fertility rate was *higher*, 85. From the low level of 1936, the birth rate rose to 25.3 in 1957, and the fertility rate to 123. This was the peak of the "baby boom" that resulted from births postponed during the Depression and war. Other factors were the earlier age at marriage and the greater proportion of married women in the population compared with 1936. By 1968, the fertility rate had declined to 85 and the birth rate to 17.4, the lowest ever recorded in this country. This decrease is explained in part by the fact that in the 1968 population there was a larger proportion of children not yet capable of reproduction. The current fertility rate is undoubtedly affected by the war in Vietnam.

Had the 1936 fertility rate of 75.8 been maintained, it would have led to an approximately stationary population. A fertility rate of 85, if maintained and if current rates of death, sterility, and sexual union continue, would lead to an increase in population. Such a fertility rate, continued over the full thirty-year period of fertility, would result in a total of 2,550 live births per thousand women, representing a completed family of 2.55 children per woman. Taking into account current rates of death, sterility, and sexual union, only 2.1 children per woman are needed to insure a stationary population. The difference between 2.5 and 2.1 represents an excess fertility of approximately 20 per cent above replacement level.

Ryder and Westoff have reported a 1965 poll in which 21 per cent of the respondents reported having at least one unwanted child. The 1965 National Fertility Study, quoted by Harkavy, Jaffe, and Wishik, reported that 5.7 per cent of first births were unwanted, the frequency increasing to 56.7 for sixth and later births. If these rates hold for 1968, it would not be unrealistic to believe that the number of unwanted births in this country approximates the number of those born in excess of those necessary for population replacement. Thus, unless fertility rates change, the provision of adequate total health care, including contraception and access to abortion without legal restriction, might go far toward reducing unwanted births and the threat of overpopulation in our country.

Appendix III

Reproductive Processes and Fertility Control

To RELATE METHODS of birth control to the process of reproduction, we list below the series of events that lead to the production of a human being, beginning at the point at which sex cells reach maturity.

1. Maturation of sex cells.
2. Release of ovum or sperm.
3. Travel of ovum or sperm to Fallopian tube.
4. Penetration of ovum by sperm, fertilization.
5. Cell division of fertilized ovum (zygote).
6. Implantation of resulting group of cells (blastocyst) in wall of uterus.
7. Development of embryo.
8. Growth of fetus.
9. Quickening (stage at which mother first feels movement).
10. Viability (ability of fetus to survive outside uterus).
11. Birth.

89

Methods of Contraception

Pills

The oral contraceptives in current use are similar to one another in principle. They are combinations of a pregnancy hormone (progestogen) and a female hormone (estrogen). They act by suppressing stage 2 above. They are available only by prescription, and should be taken under a physician's direction.

The *pill* is the most effective method of contraception known. It is convenient, cheap, and aesthetically acceptable because its use is separated from the sexual act.

The side effects and possible dangers of using the pill arise from the fact that the physiological changes of pregnancy are imitated to some extent. Some women find these pregnancy-like sensations distasteful, while others report that they have never felt better. The most serious reaction, extremely rare, is the formation of a blood clot, which may lodge in the lungs or brain. One British study found an incidence of three deaths from this cause per hundred thousand women taking the pill.

The *post-coital pill* acts by preventing stage 6. Large doses of estrogenic substances, if taken the week following intercourse, have been thought by some to interrupt or prevent implantation. The medication is in an experimental state, is not recommended for regular use, but is prescribed by some doctors in cases of rape or incest.

Intrauterine Devices (IUD's)

The presence within the uterus of a foreign body has long been known to prevent pregnancy. It is only recently that perfection of plastics and stainless steel has made the method attractive. Exactly how the device acts is not yet known, but recent research suggests that it induces within the womb the release of an enzyme that prevents pregnancy.

IUD's are coils, rings, spirals, or loops made in various shapes and sizes. They must be inserted in the uterus by a physician or a specially trained nurse or midwife. Some 10 per cent to 30 per cent of women cannot tolerate the device, and it is either spontaneously expelled or must be removed because of pain or bleeding. When retained, protection against pregnancy is second only to that afforded by the pill.

The IUD has major advantages. The woman need not concern herself about contraception, except for an occasional check for the presence of the device. (This is done by feeling for the thin, flexible plastic threads that are attached to most such devices and are left trailing out of the cervical canal into the vagina.) The IUD can be removed when a woman wants to have children. It is cheap.

IUD's are safer than the pill. On extremely rare occasions, the device may perforate the uterus and lodge in the abdominal cavity. In only a few instances have deaths been attributed to the IUD.

Mechanical Barriers

Prior to the development of the pill and the IUD, the most popular contraceptive used by females was the *diaphragm*. This is a shallow rubber cup that is inserted in the vagina so as to cover the cervix (entrance to the uterus) and the wall around the cervix. It must be supplemented by a sperm-killing cream or jelly, since the main purpose of the diaphragm is to hold the sperm-killer against the opening of the cervix.

Properly used, the diaphragm is effective. But slips often occur, so that protection against pregnancy is not so good as that achieved by the pill or the IUD.

The objections to the diaphragm are that it is messy and that since it must be inserted either daily before bedtime or before intercourse, it requires the woman to plan ahead, thus detracting from the spontaneity of sex relations.

The *condom,* or male sheath, similarly acts as a mechanical barrier. It is the device most widely used by men. Like the diaphragm, it is effective when properly used, but slips occur often enough to make it less effective than the pill or the IUD. The advantages are cheapness, availability, and the absence of need for medical advice. Many men, however, find the condom objectionable because they say it lessens sexual pleasure.

Spermatocides

Substances that kill or immobilize sperm, preventing stage 3, may be inserted into the vagina before intercourse. Creams and aerosol foams are injected with a special applicator shortly before intercourse. They are reasonably effective for a short period of time. Jellies and tablets are somewhat less protective. All require intelligence and forethought and must be inserted shortly before intercourse. Most of these products are more expensive than condoms.

Rhythm

The rhythm method, or periodic continence (also called "the safe period" method), is the only method of birth control, other than total abstinence, currently sanctioned by the Roman Catholic Church. It depends completely on self-control and is based on the sequence of events in the female menstrual cycle. Usually a woman's fertile period (the time when an egg cell is released by one of her ovaries) occurs twelve to sixteen days before menstruation. Strictly speaking, a woman is fertile only for the few hours (less than twenty-four) following ovulation. Intercourse subsequent to this period does not result in pregnancy. Intercourse preceding it may result in pregnancy, because sperm have a longer life than ova, amounting to at least four days and perhaps occasionally to as long as seven days. A fertile period as short as seven days cannot be counted upon, however, because ovulation is not regular and cannot be predicted or dated with accuracy. Accuracy in dating ovulation can be increased by a daily record of the woman's body temperature, which shows changes at and after ovulation. The method requires a high degree of self-control and the keeping of an accurate calendar and daily record of body temperature. Even with strict adherence to the necessary regimen, this is by far the least effective of methods currently prescribed by doctors.

Coitus Interruptus (withdrawal of the penis from the vagina before the man reaches his climax)

This method is also based on self-control. Even when men are motivated and determined to prevent conception, however, they are not always successful. Sometimes the climax comes before they expect it, or semen escapes before the climax. Nevertheless, this is said to be the most common method in use in Europe today and to be responsible for the decline in birth rates during the eighteenth, nineteenth, and twentieth centuries.

Research in Contraception

The ideal contraceptive is still to be developed. Research is being conducted vigorously in many laboratories to eliminate the side effects and other disadvantages of the contraceptives now in use. These experiments include: the elimination of estrogen from oral contraceptives; long-term injections of progestin, effective for three months; the insertion under the skin of a capsule that slowly leaks progestin into the body fluids, effective for several years; once-a-month pills; the "morning-after" pill, to prevent implantation of the fertilized ovum in the uterus; compounds to be taken, when pregnancy is suspected, to induce menstruation and thus dislodge the product of conception.

Abortion

According to the American College of Obstetricians and Gynecologists, pregnancy begins with implantation of the fertilized ovum (stage 6 above), and abortion (the termination of pregnancy) is the removal of the product of conception. Abortions are usually performed during the first three months of pregnancy, before quickening, using methods described on page 30.

Sterilization

Neither female sterilization (tubal ligation) nor male sterilization (vasectomy) is completely successful in preventing pregnancy. The failure rate, according to ten major studies, is about 1 per cent. Since there is no guarantee that surgical sterilization can be reversed, it is recommended only for those who are certain that they do not want more children or should not have them.

When a tubal ligation is performed, a small abdominal incision is made and the woman's Fallopian tubes are cut and tied. The operation is simple if performed soon after the delivery of a child.

Vasectomy is a minor operation, under local anesthesia, that does not require hospitalization. Severing the sperm-carrying tubes is performed through a small incision in the upper scrotum, and the man can return to work the following day.

Neither type of sterilization adversely affects pleasure in sex relations.

Appendix IV

Positions on Abortion

Roman Catholic

THE ROMAN CATHOLIC CHURCH currently holds that a new life begins at conception and therefore forbids destruction of an embryo or fetus except in cases of indirect abortion when a remedy is used to effect a cure of a disease or condition of the mother likely to be fatal, which incidentally causes the death of the unborn child.

The Church's teaching is based on Canon 2350, on the action of Pope Benedict XV in 1917, and on the encyclical *Casti Connubi,* issued by Pope Pius XI in 1930. The encyclical states that "the life of each (mother and fetus) is equally sacred and no one has the power, not even the public authority, to destroy it." (The encyclical also condemns any deliberate "limitation of the generation of offspring" as an "act against nature.")

In his encyclical *Humanae Vitae,* issued in 1968, Pope Paul VI said:

We must once again declare that the direct interruption of the generative process already begun, and above all, directly willed and procured abortion, even if for therapeutic reasons, are to be absolutely excluded as licit means of regulating birth.

Protestant

The National Council of Churches, in 1961, approved hospital abortion "when the health or life of the mother is at stake." It stressed the sanctity of potential life and condemned abortion as a method of birth control.

Positions of individual Protestant denominations vary. Generally, abortion is tolerated when the health or life of the mother is threatened. Some denominational policy statements are given below.

American Baptist Convention (resolution adopted at meetings May 29–June 1, 1968) "recognizes that abortion should be a matter of responsible personal decision" and urges legislation to provide that (1) the ending of a pregnancy before the twelfth week "be at the request of the individual(s) concerned and be regarded as an elective medical procedure governed by the laws regulating medical practice and licensure," and (2) after that period a pregnancy be terminated "only by a duly licensed physician at the request of the individual(s) concerned" for reasons suggested by the Model Penal Code of the American Law Institute (substantial risk to physical or mental health of the mother; risk that the child would be born with grave physical or mental defect; rape, incest, or other felonious acts as the cause of the pregnancy).

"Further, we encourage our churches to provide sympathetic and realistic counseling on family planning and abortion.

"We commend study, research, and development of understanding on the part of the populace led by the people of our churches toward an enlightened view of this provocative problem."

Protestant Episcopal Church and Church of England (Lambeth Conference, 1958) allowed abortion at the dictate of strict and undeniable medical necessity, broad enough to cover health as well as life.   '

A more recent statement of the Department of Christian Social Relations of the Episcopal Church stated that abortion is probably decided among Episcopalians on the basis of the moral judgment of the individual, her family, the parish priest, and her physician.

In October 1965 a committee of the Board for Social Responsibility of the Church of England declared that:

. . . the problem of abortion is precisely the problem of weighing the claims of the mother against the claims of the fetus and _vice versa,_ when they conflict, though it is important that neither be thought of in isolation from the family group of which they are a part.

. . . in certain circumstances abortion can be justified. This would be when, at the request of the mother and after the kind of consultation which we have envisaged (the pooling of the knowledge and judgments of the general practitioner, a psychiatric or other consultant, a medical social worker, a psychiatric social worker, or other person professionally interested in the case), it could be reasonably established that there was a threat to the mother's life or well-being, and hence inescapably to her health, if she were obliged to carry the child to term and give it birth. And our view is that, in reaching this conclusion, her life and well being must be seen as integrally connected with the life and well being of her family.

[The] consultative procedure would cover those cases where justification for abortion would rest upon there being an assessable risk of a defective or deformed child, as well as cases of incest or rape; though the ground of the decision would be the prognosis concerning the mother as affected by the pregnancy in question; not the possibility of deformity itself, not simply the fact (if established) of the act of incest or of rape. . . . [The suggested consultation, in cases where abortion is not indicated,] would give the patient access to the skilled medical and social services which can afford her the encouragement, help and support which she may need to continue the pregnancy and give birth to the child.

Unitarian Universalist Association (1968 General Assembly) "urges that efforts be made to abolish existing abortion laws, except to prohibit performance of an abortion by a person who is not a duly licensed physician, leaving the decision as to an abortion to the doctor and his patient."

United Presbyterian Church (1962 General Assembly): "One of the issues often discussed is the question of priority as to saving the mother's life or the child's life. This must be decided on the basis of the specific medical problems involved."

Jewish

Jewish positions on abortion vary among Orthodox, Conservative, and Reform groups. In no case is it completely prohibited. The Orthodox group takes the most restrictive position, the Reform the most radical.

The Union of American Hebrew Congregations (November 11–16, 1967) spoke out in the name of its United States members "in favor of needed revisions in the abortion laws of many states. . . ."

We commend those states which have enacted humane legislation in this area and we appeal to other states to do likewise and permit abortions under such circumstances as threatened disease or deformity of the embryo or fetus, threats to the physical and mental health of the mother, rape and incest, and the social, economic and psychological factors that might warrant therapeutic termination of pregnancy.

We urge our constituent congregations to join with other forward-looking citizens in securing needed revisions and liberalization of abortion laws.

American Medical Association
(Policy Adopted in June 1967)

. . . the American Medical Association is opposed to induced abortion except when:

1. There is documented medical evidence that continuance of the pregnancy may threaten the health or life of the mother, or

2. There is documented medical evidence that the infant may be born with incapacitating physical deformity or mental deficiency, or

3. There is documented medical evidence that continuance of a pregnancy, resulting from legally established statutory or forcible rape or incest may constitute a threat to the mental or physical health of the patient;

4. Two other physicians chosen because of their recognized professional competence have examined the patient and have concurred in writing; and

5. The procedure is performed in a hospital accredited by the Joint Commission on Accreditation of Hospitals.

The American College of Obstetricians
and Gynecologists (May 9, 1968)

. . . First, the American College of Obstetricians and Gynecologists regards therapeutic or medical abortion as primarily a medical responsibility. Secondly, any law concerned with therapeutic abortion should view as relevant that excessive numbers of pregnancies and resultant offspring may cause social and economic erosion of the family. . . .

In broadening the law to take into account the patient's entire environment, actual or reasonably foreseeable, in assessing maternal risk, the medical profession must consider and give thoughtful evaluation to each individual request. Experience will support the concept that physicians can convince patients to continue an unplanned pregnancy provided steps will be taken to prevent future unwanted pregnancy; and society should provide the necessary economic support for the patient so that she will continue and complete the pregnancy.

. . . the College will not condone nor support the concept that an abortion be considered or performed for any unwanted pregnancy or as a means of population control. It is emphasized that the inherent risk of such an abortion is not fully appreciated both by many in the profession and certainly not by the public. Where abortion may be obtained on demand, as in Japan and the Soviet Union, medical authorities of both these nations indicate that the physical and psychological sequelae are still to be determined. Moreover, where abortion is so practiced it can be said that the mortality and morbidity rates are difficult to ascertain. Further, the public should realize that in countries or societies that permit abortion on demand, many, if not the majority, are performed in physicians' offices. Under these circumstances, it is reasonable to conclude that the mortality from this operation may exceed the maternal mortality of the United States and Canada while the incidence of serious complications is substantial.

Termination of pregnancy by therapeutic abortion is a medical procedure. It must be performed only in a hospital accredited by the Joint Commission on Accreditation of Hospitals and by a licensed physician qualified to perform such operations.

Therapeutic abortion is permitted only with the informed consent of the patient and her husband, or herself if unmarried, or of her nearest relative if she is under the age of consent. No patient should be compelled to undergo, or a physician to perform, a therapeutic abortion if either has ethical, religious or any other objections to it.

A consultative opinion must be obtained from at least two licensed physicians other than the one who is to perform the procedure. This opinion should state that the procedure is medically indicated. The consultants may act separately or as a special committee. One consultant should be a qualified obstetrician-gynecologist and one should have special competence in the medical area in which the medical indications for the procedure reside.

Therapeutic abortion may be performed for the following established medical indications:

1. When continuation of the pregnancy may threaten the life of the woman or seriously impair her health. In determining whether or not there is such risk to health, account may be taken of the patient's total environment, actual or reasonably foreseeable.
2. When pregnancy has resulted from rape or incest; in this case the same medical criteria should be employed in the evaluation of the patient.
3. When continuation of the pregnancy is likely to result in the birth of a child with grave physical deformities or mental retardation.

American Psychiatric Association
(Resolution of June 1967)

This resolution recognized that "pregnancy can constitute a grave threat to the life or mental health of certain women with emotional or mental illness or disordered emotional development" and "to the mental health of certain prospective mothers" and approved abortion on medical grounds for the same reasons as those outlined in the model code of the American Law Institute (page 105).*

American Public Health Association
(Resolution Adopted at Annual Conference, November 1968)

This resolution is based on a belief in the right of individuals to decide the number and spacing of their children, and recognition that contraceptives are not always obtainable, used, or, if used, always effective.

. . . safe legal abortion should be available to all women. Further, the provision of abortion within the usual channels of medical care will reduce the well-known adverse health effects of illegal abortion.

* See also "The Right to Abortion: A Psychiatric View." Report of the Committee on Psychiatry and Law of the Group for the Advancement of Psychiatry. Vol. 7, No. 75 (October 1969).

The APHA urges that access to abortion be accepted as an important means of securing the right to spacing and choosing the number of children wanted. To this end, restrictive laws should be repealed so that pregnant women may have abortions performed by qualified practitioners of medicine and osteopathy.

Physicians' Forum
(Statement Adopted in 1968)

The statement of the Physicians' Forum points out the limitations of the suggested model code of the American Law Institute and "holds that every woman has the right to regulate her reproductive life"; that "the decision regarding abortion is a highly individual matter which should be agreed upon by patient and physician"; and that "abortion is a medical concern." It urges "the repeal of all laws which accept the premise that abortion is a criminal act."

Planned Parenthood–World Population
(Statement Adopted in 1968 by the
National Medical Advisory Committee)

1. The National Medical Advisory Committee of Planned Parenthood–World Population believes that it is the right of every woman to decide without coercion of any sort whether and when to have a child.

2. The Committee reaffirms that abortion is a medical procedure, the decision for which must rest with the woman and her physician.

3. This decision should be made with full knowledge of the woman's personal situation, with consideration of her physical and psychological condition and her social, economic, and cultural environment.

4. The Committee therefore recommends the abolition of existing statutes and criminal laws regarding abortion when performed by properly qualified physicians with reasonable medical safeguards, and the recognition that advice, counseling, and referral with regard to abortion are integral parts of medical care.

American Civil Liberties Union
(Statement Adopted in March 1968)

. . . The violations of civil liberties inherent in the present abortion laws are sharply accentuated by the immense medical and social problems to which these laws have given rise. . . .

[Although these problems] are without doubt extremely serious, in pressing for legislative abolition of the abortion laws the Union bases its arguments solely on its desire to protect and promote the civil liberties of all citizens. We believe that the abortion laws violate civil liberties in the following specific ways:

1. They deprive women of the liberty to decide whether and when their bodies are to be used for procreation, without due process of law.
2. They are unconstitutionally vague.
3. They deny to women in the lower economic groups the equal protection of the laws guaranteed by the Fourteenth Amendment, since abortions are now freely available to the rich but unobtainable by the poor.
4. They infringe upon the right to decide whether and when to have a child, as well as the marital right of privacy.
5. They impair the right of physicians to practice in accordance with their professional obligations in that they require doctors not to perform a necessary medical procedure. In many cases their failure to perform this medical procedure because of the statutory prohibitions on abortion would amount to malpractice.

General Federation of Women's Clubs
(Resolution Adopted in June 1969)

WHEREAS, The members of the General Federation of Women's Clubs are deeply concerned in all matters that involve the lives and welfare of women, children and the family as a whole; and

WHEREAS, The General Federation of Women's Clubs feels that laws governing therapeutic abortion are of tremendous importance to women and the family; and

WHEREAS, The General Federation of Women's Clubs respects the belief of those who on moral or religious grounds oppose therapeutic abortions under any circumstances; and

WHEREAS, The General Federation of Women's Clubs is also concerned with the increasing problem of caring for children and adults who are severely impaired physically and mentally; and

WHEREAS, The legal and medical professions, after careful study, have arrived at safeguards that would prevent the possibility of "abortion on demand"; therefore

RESOLVED, That the General Federation of Women's Clubs declares its conviction that therapeutic abortion should be permitted when:

1. There is documented medical evidence that continuance of a pregnancy threatens the health or life of the mother; or
2. There is documented medical evidence that the infant is likely to be born with severe and permanent physical deformity or mental deficiency; or
3. There is documented medical evidence that continuance of a pregnancy resulting from legally established statutory or forcible rape or incest is likely to constitute a threat to the mental or physical health of the patient; and
4. Two physicians (other than the attending) chosen because of their professional competence have examined the patient and have concurred in writing in the advisability of therapeutic abortion; and
5. The procedure is performed in a hospital accredited by the Joint Commission on Accreditation of Hospitals; and further

RESOLVED, That the General Federation of Women's Clubs urges its member clubs to study laws governing abortion in their respective states and to work for their modification in relation to therapeutic abortion consistent with their conviction.

Appendix V

Abortion Laws

Model Penal Code of The American Law Institute* (Proposed Official Draft, May 4, 1962)

Section 230.3. Abortion

1. *Unjustified Abortion*. A person who purposely and unjustifiably terminates the pregnancy of another otherwise than by a live birth commits a felony of the third degree or, where the pregnancy has continued beyond the twenty-sixth week, a felony of the second degree.

2. *Justifiable Abortion*. A licensed physician is justified in terminating a pregnancy if he believes there is substantial risk that continuance of the pregnancy would gravely impair the physical or mental health of the mother or that the child would be born with

grave physical or mental defect, or that the pregnancy resulted from rape, incest, or other felonious intercourse. All illicit intercourse with a girl below the age of 16 shall be deemed felonious for purposes of this Subsection. Justifiable abortions shall be performed only in a licensed hospital except in case of emergency when hospital facilities are unavailable. [Additional exceptions from the requirement of hospitalization may be incorporated here to take account of situations in sparsely settled areas where hospitals are not generally accessible.]

3. *Physicians' Certificates; Presumption from Non-Compliance.* No abortion shall be performed unless two physicians, one of whom may be the person performing the abortion, shall have certified in writing the circumstances which they believe to justify the abortion. Such certificate shall be submitted before the abortion to the hospital where it is to be performed and, in the case of abortion following felonious intercourse, to the prosecuting attorney or the police. Failure to comply with any of the requirements of this Subsection gives rise to a presumption that the abortion was unjustified.

4. *Self-Abortion.* A woman whose pregnancy has continued beyond the twenty-sixth week commits a felony of the third degree if she purposely terminates her own pregnancy otherwise than by a live birth, or if she uses instruments, drugs or violence upon herself for that purpose. Except as justified under Subsection 2, a person who induces or knowingly aids a woman to use instruments, drugs or violence upon herself for the purpose of terminating her pregnancy otherwise than by a live birth commits a felony of the third degree whether or not the pregnancy has continued beyond the twenty-sixth week.

5. *Pretended Abortion.* A person commits a felony of the third degree if, representing that it is his purpose to perform an abortion, he does an act adapted to cause abortion in a pregnant woman although the woman is in fact not pregnant, or the actor does not believe she is. A person charged with unjustified abortion under Subsection 1 or an attempt to commit that offense may be convicted thereof upon proof of conduct prohibited by this Subsection.

6. *Distribution of Abortifacients.* A person who sells, offers to sell, possesses with intent to sell, advertises, or displays for sale anything specially designed to terminate a pregnancy, or held out by the actor as useful for that purpose, commits a misdemeanor, unless:

a. the sale, offer, or display is to a physician or druggist or to an intermediary in a chain of distribution to physicians or druggists; or

b. the sale is made upon prescription or order of a physician; or

c. the possession is with intent to sell as authorized in paragraphs (a) and (b); or

d. the advertising is addressed to persons named in paragraph (a) and confined to trade or professional channels not likely to reach the general public.

7. *Section Inapplicable to Prevention of Pregnancy.* Nothing in this Section shall be deemed applicable to the prescription, administration, or distribution of drugs or other substances for avoiding pregnancy, whether by preventing implantation of a fertilized ovum or by any other method that operates before, at, or immediately after fertilization.

TABLE 2   MAJOR PROVISIONS OF NEW STATE LAWS ON ABORTION

Legal Provisions	Miss. 1966	Colo. 1967	N.C. 1967	Cal. 1967	Ga. 1968	Md. 1968	Ark. 1969	N.M. 1969	Kans. 1969	Ore. 1969	Del. 1969
Grounds for abortion											
Preserve life of mother	x	x	x		x		x	x			x
Preserve physical health of mother		x	health	x	health		health	x	x[1]	x[1]	x
Preserve mental health of mother		x	health	x	health		health	x	x[1]	x[1]	x
Psychiatric confirmation required		x									
Risk of serious physical or mental defect in child		x	x[2]	x	x		x[2]	x	x		x
Rape	x	x	x[2]	x	x		x[2]	x	x		x
Affidavit of mother required				x	x						
Statement of district attorney or court official required				x	x						
Incest		x	x[3]	x	x		x[2]	x	x		x[3]
Felonious intercourse		x									x
Duration of pregnancy											
Less than 16 weeks in case of rape		x		x							
Not more than 20 weeks						x[4]					
Not more than 150 days										x[5]	
Not more than 26 weeks											x[4]

Provision						
Residence requirement						
Resident of state				X		
4 months except in emergency	X					X
4 months with other exceptions	X					
Request or consent						
Woman		X				X
Woman and husband if living together		X			X	
Parents of unmarried minor	X	X				X
Parents or guardian of incompetent	X					X
Approval or authorization						
Hospital review board	X	X	X	X		X
Certification by three doctors			X		X[5]	
Certification by two doctors	X					X[6]

1 In determining "substantial risk" to the woman's health, account may be taken of her "total environment, actual or reasonably foreseeable."

2 Provided it is reported to a law enforcement official within seven days.

3 Not required if abortion is performed within 48 hours after the alleged rape.

4 Unless mother's life is in danger or the fetus is dead.

5 Unless mother's life is in danger.

6 In cases not involving rape.

Appendix VI

New Definitions of Death

THE TRADITIONAL MEDICAL STANDARD for determining the time of death, accepted by the law, has been the definition of death in *Black's Law Dictionary*:

The cessation of life; the ceasing to exist; defined by physicians as a total stoppage of the circulation of the blood and a cessation of the animal and vital functions consequent thereon, such as respiration, pulsation, etc.

Now that physicians can revive the heart after it has stopped beating, a new definition of death has become necessary. Many medical authorities no longer believe that this definition should be based on the cessation of heartbeat and respiration.

New criteria for death, centering on death of the brain, currently are under wide discussion (see Ref. G 1, G 17, and G 22 of the Bibliography). The most acceptable definition of brain death to date has been that set forth by the Ad Hoc Committee of the Harvard Medical School under the title,

110

"A Definition of Irreversible Coma" (Ref. G 22). Their criteria are:

1. Unreceptivity and unresponsivity (that is, no response even to painful stimuli).
2. No muscular movement and no spontaneous breathing for at least one hour, or for three minutes if a mechanical respirator is turned off.
3. No elicitable reflexes, ocular movements, or blinking, and the presence of fixed dilated pupils.
4. A flat isoelectric electroencephalogram (EEG).
5. No change when all of these tests are repeated at least twenty-four hours later.
6. These criteria to be exclusive of two conditions: hypothermia (body temperature below 90° F.) or central nervous system depression due to drugs such as barbiturates.

To these criteria Dr. Francis Moore adds that of obvious gross major structural damage to the head (G 29).

Most physicians believe that the determination of death is a matter for medical decision and not for codification by law (G 25).

Medical debate over the new definition of death appears to center around the length of time that cessation of brain activity must continue before death can be certified, since it is possible for brain wave activity to resume after it has stopped. This question is especially difficult where heart transplants are involved, for the organ must be removed as soon as possible after death and the twenty-four hours specified in the Harvard definition may be too long a delay for the heart to remain in usable condition.

Appendix VII

Laws Concerning the Donation of Tissues and Organs

The United States

A MODEL ACT, to facilitate the donation and use of human tissues and organs for transplantation and other medical purposes, was approved by the National Conference of the Commissioners on Uniform State Laws in July 1968 and was endorsed by the American Bar Association and the American Medical Association. By early 1969 legislation based on this act had been proposed or made law in thirty-five states. According to an Associated Press survey, eleven other states covered some of the same legal questions.

The need for such a law stems from the problems inherent in the use of an organ or tissue in another person after the death of the donor. The law in the past has tried to recognize four interests that often are conflicting: (1) the wishes of the deceased, (2) the wishes of the surviving spouse or next of kin, (3) the need for organs, tissues, and cadavers for medical education, research, and therapy including transplantation, and (4) the need of society to determine the cause of death in certain circumstances.

The Uniform Anatomical Gift Act attempts to reconcile these conflicting interests. It states who may execute such an anatomical gift (anyone in sound mind and eighteen years of age or over may specify the gift ahead of time to take effect on death, or in the absence of such specification, persons in successive gradation of kinship may give permission, provided the decedent had not given definite notice to the contrary). The act states who may receive such gifts and for what purposes (accredited hospitals, medical schools, tissue and organ banks, surgeons, physicians, or any specified individual for treatment or transplantation needed by him). The wish to make the gift may be made by will or on a card carried on the person, and may be revoked by the donor at any time.

The act states that the time of death shall be determined by the physician who attends the donor at the time of death, and that this physician shall not participate in the procedures for transplantation.

For the exact text of the act and commentary on it, the reader should consult Reference G 27 in the Bibliography.

Other Countries

The legal status of comparable procedures in countries other than the United States varies widely; these have been concisely reviewed in "a survey of existing legislation" by the World Health Organization (Reference G 28 in the Bibliography). France would appear to be the most liberal: There an organ may be removed from the deceased immediately without authorization by the family (or the decedent) if the physician in charge believes it to be in the interest of science or therapeutics. In Denmark and the United Kingdom, organs or tissues may be removed promptly if the deceased had given prior consent in writing or if he had expressed no objection and the nearest relatives have expressed none. In South Africa, a magistrate may give such permission.

Many model acts are now being considered in Canada and other Commonwealth countries, as well as elsewhere in the world. For details the reader is referred to the reference cited above.

Bibliography

THE FOLLOWING BOOKS AND ARTICLES are listed here for the benefit
of the reader who may wish to explore further some or all aspects
of the subject of this book. These lists also indicate some of the
sources of fact and opinion on which the members of the Working
Party have drawn in formulating their own thoughts on these difficult problems.

These lists are by no means complete, but they do provide a
beginning; most of the books and articles provide many more
references to other writings. Books listed in the first section, en-
titled "General Reading," for the most part cover all the subjects
under discussion in this present work and hence overlap many of
the books and articles listed subsequently in separate categories.

For the convenience of the general reader who wishes a less ex-
haustive and scholarly guide to further reading, the references
thought to be most useful and readable are marked with an asterisk.
To help the reader further in his choice, some, though not all, references are briefly annotated.

Although all the members of the Working Party contributed to
this bibliography, one member (J. R. Elkinton) is primarily responsible for its organization and for the preparation of most of
the annotations.

115

A. General Reading

1. FLETCHER, Joseph, *Morals and Medicine*. Boston, Beacon Press, Inc., 1960. A forthright statement by an Episcopal clergyman of a liberal approach to the moral problems of contraception, artificial insemination, sterilization, euthanasia, and the patient's right to die with dignity; all based on the sanctity of the human personality.

* 2. WOLSTENHOLME, G. E. W. (ed.), *Man and His Future,* a Ciba Foundation Symposium. Boston, Little, Brown and Company, 1963. A provocative discussion of the future in terms of population, nutrition, genetics, eugenics, medicine, psychology, and the behavioral sciences. The documents include such well-known experts as Sir Julian Huxley, John Brock, Gregory Pincus, Hermann Muller, Joshua Lederberg, J. B. S. Haldane, and others.

3. DUBOS, René, *Man Adapting*. New Haven, Yale University Press, 1965, especially Chap. 11, "The Population Avalanche." A leading medical scientist and philosopher discusses the increase in man's numbers as one of the modern conditions to which we must now adapt.

4. ELKINTON, J. R. (ed.), *The Changing Mores of Biomedical Research: A Colloquium on Ethical Dilemmas from Medical Advances. Annals of Internal Medicine,* Vol. 67, Part II, Supp. 7 (September 1967). A philosopher; a judge—and future Chief Justice of the Supreme Court; a psychologist; two geneticist-biologists—both Nobel Laureates; a pharmacologist; a microbiologist; a surgeon; and three physicians discuss the legal, social, ethical, and scientific dilemmas of contraception, abortion, human experimentation, chemical manipulation of the mind, transplantation of organs, and eugenics.

5. COMPSTON, Nigel D. (ed.), *The Cost of Life,* Symposium Number 9. *Proceedings of the Royal Society of Medicine,* 60 (November 1967), II, 1195. Again, a stimulating multidisciplinary discussion by British experts of the legal, social, and ethical dilemmas in abortion, in the care of malformed and mentally subnormal children, and in prolongation of the lives of the elderly and the dying.

6. EDMUNDS, V., and C. G. Scorer (eds.), *Ethical Responsibility in Medicine. A Christian Approach.* Baltimore, The Williams and Wilkins Company, 1967. A group of essays by British doctors and a Church of England clergyman, presenting a liberal and open-minded application of Christian principles to the problems of birth, death, alcoholism, and drug addiction.

* 7. ROBERTS, Catherine, *The Scientific Conscience: Reflections on the Modern Biologist and Humanism.* New York, George Braziller, 1967. An unusual set of essays by a microbiologist who has become concerned over the failure of biological science to recognize its ethical limitations and the moral consequences of its advances. Positive eugenics versus psychosocial evolution is discussed in the light of the need for spiritual values.

* 8. BERRILL, N. J., *The Person in the Womb.* New York, Dodd, Mead & Company, 1968. A humane, philosophical, and eminent developmental biologist presents with elegant simplicity the stages of, and hazards to, the developing new human life. The problems of population control, abortion, and genetic counseling and manipulation are set in the perspective of evolution. "No child must be born without a hope, no woman must bear a child against her will and the sons of men must not overwhelm the earth."

9. LABBY, Daniel H. (ed.), *Life or Death: Ethics and Options.* Seattle, University of Washington Press, 1968. A sociologist, a lawyer, a theologian, a biologist, a philosopher, and a physician address themselves to the question of the place in modern biomedical science of the concept of the sanctity of life.

* 10. TORREY, E. Fuller (ed.), *Ethical Issues in Medicine. The Role of the Physician in Today's Society.* Boston, Little, Brown and Company, 1968. Twenty physicians present succinct essays on all the subjects of this book—from Catholic and Protestant points of view—and on medical issues in war and poverty as well.

11. LASAGNA, Louis, *Life, Death, and the Doctor.* New York, Alfred A. Knopf, Inc., 1968. A detailed and comprehensive book written for the layman by a liberal physician on the

Johns Hopkins faculty. Covers not only the subjects of this
book but also the adequacy of the doctor's training and
the relationships between medicine and the law.

B. The Population Problem

Books and Pamphlets

* 1. MUDD, Stuart (ed.), *The Population Crisis and the Use of
World Resources.* The Hague, Dr. W. Junk, Publishers;
Bloomington, Indiana University Press, 1964. An anthology
compiled for the World Academy of Art and Science,
written by prominent thinkers and experts in many fields.
The opening essays by Adlai Stevenson, Bertrand Russell,
and Julian Huxley stress the importance of the problems
that are dealt with in the rest of the book. Here are
probably more detailed facts and thoughtful expositions of
all aspects of the population problem in every part of the
world, and of the relevant resources of the world, than are
to be found in any other single volume of comparable size.
Quite rightly, the central theme is the concern for values
and the quality of future human life; the ancient truth is
reasserted: Man does not live by bread alone.
2. NG, Larry K. Y., and Stuart Mudd (eds.), *The Population
Crisis.* Bloomington, Indiana University Press, 1965. An
abridged and revised paperback edition of the book listed
in Ref. B 1.
3. PETERSON, W., *Population.* New York, The Macmillan Company, 1961.
4. BROWN, Harrison, *The Challenge of Man's Future.* New York,
The Viking Press, Inc., 1963.
5. *The Growth of World Population. Analysis of the Problems
and Recommendations for Research and Training.* National Academy of Sciences—National Research Council,
Publication 1091. Washington, D. C., 1963.
6. FREEDMAN, Ronald, *Population: The Vital Revolution.* New
York, Doubleday and Company, Inc., 1964.
7. HAUSER, P. M. (ed.), *The Population Dilemma.* Englewood
Cliffs, N. J., Prentice-Hall, Inc., 1965.

8. *The World Food Problem: Report of the President's Science Advisory Committee 1967*. Washington, D. C., U. S. Government Printing Office, 1967. 3 vols.

9. YOUNG, Louise B., *Population in Perspective*. New York, Oxford University Press, 1968.

* 10. RAULET, Harry M., *Family Planning and Population Control in Developing Countries*. Institute of International Agriculture, College of Agriculture and Natural Resources, Misc. No. 4. East Lansing, Michigan State University, 1968. A wise and scholarly monograph, pointing out that population growth is not necessarily a limiting factor in economic growth, questioning the neo-Malthusian outlook, and suggesting that education, health, nutrition, etc. may be crucial to economic growth and should not be slighted for family planning programs of dubious effectiveness.

11. LUCAS, F. L., "The Greatest Problem of Today," in F. L. Lucas, *The Greatest Problem and Other Essays*. New York, The Macmillan Company, 1961. A lucid and elegant essay by one of the great literary dons of Cambridge University, stressing the importance of preserving values and the quality of human life.

* 12. HUXLEY, Sir Julian, (a) "The Impending Crisis," in Ref. B. 1, pp. 6–11; (b) "The Crowded World," in Sir Julian Huxley, *Essays of a Humanist*. London, Chatto & Windus, 1964, pp. 241–250. Two penetrating statements of the population problem by one of the world's most famous biologists and former Director General of UNESCO.

13. STEWART, Maxwell S., *A New Look at Our Crowded World*. *Public Affairs Pamphlet* No. 393, 1966.

14. EHRLICH, Paul R., *The Population Bomb*. New York, Ballantine Books, 1968.

15. *Population Crisis*. Hearings before the Subcommittee on Foreign Aid Expenditures of the Committee on Government Operations, United States Senate, Sessions on S. 1676 (A Bill to Reorganize the Department of State and the Department of Health, Education, and Welfare). 89th Congress, First Session, 1965; Second Session, 1966; 90th Congress, First Session, 1967; Second Session, 1968. Washington, D. C. U. S. Government Printing Office.

* 16. SNOW, C. P., *The State of Siege*. New York, Charles Scribner's Sons, 1969.

17. *World Population—A Challenge to the United Nations and Its System of Agencies.* Report of National Policy Panel established by the United Nations Association of the United States of America, May 1969.

Articles

18. FOX, Sir Theodore, "The Multiplication of Man or Noah's New Flood." *The Lancet,* 2 (1966), 1238. An able and readable exposition of the problem with special reference to England and to the interesting question of optimal, as opposed to maximal, population. By the distinguished former editor of *The Lancet.*

19. DAY, Richard, "Society's Stake in Responsible Parenthood." *American Journal of Diseases of Children,* 113 (1967), 519.

20. GREEP, Roy O., "Prevalence of People." *Perspectives in Biology and Medicine,* 12 (1969), 332. A clear and succinct statement of the problem and its consequences.

21. KIEFER, David M., "Population—Technology's Desperate Race with Fertility," Parts I & II. *Chemical & Engineering News,* 46, (October 1968), 118–144 and 90–107.

22. HORNADAY, Mary, "Battling the Population Bulge," *Christian Science Monitor,* December 14, 1967, p. 1.

23. MAYER, Jean, "Toward a Non-Malthusian Population Policy." *Columbia Forum,* Summer 1969, pp. 5–13. A leading nutritional scientist states his belief that the limiting factor to expanding population is not food production but exhaustion of other natural resources and a livable environment. For this reason, not the poor countries but the rich countries are in more imminent danger and for them the crisis of overpopulation has already arrived.

C. Contraception, Abortion, and Family Planning

Books and Pamphlets

* 1. CALDERONE, Mary S. (ed.), *Abortion in the United States.* New York, Harper & Row, Publishers, 1958. Papers given a

decade ago at a conference sponsored by Planned Parenthood Federation of America, Inc., and the New York
Academy of Medicine, and, sad to say, still largely relevant.
2. HIMES, Norman E., *Medical History of Contraception*. New
York, Gamut Press, Inc., 1963.
3. GUTTMACHER, A. (ed.), *The Case for Legalized Abortion Now*.
Berkeley, Calif., Diablo Press, 1967.
4. LADER, Lawrence, *Abortion*. New York, The Bobbs-Merrill
Company, Inc., 1966.
5. ROSEN, Harold (ed.), *Abortion in America*. Boston, Beacon
Press, Inc., 1967.
* 6. SMITH, David T. (ed.), *Abortion and the Law*. Cleveland,
The Press of Western Reserve University, 1967. A comprehensive discussion of current abortion laws, various religious
views, and psychiatric implications.
7. SHAW, Russell, *Abortion on Trial*. Dayton, Ohio, George A.
Pflaum, Publisher, Inc., 1968.
8. *Abortion: An Ethical Discussion*. The Church Assembly
Board for Social Responsibility, Church Information Office,
London, 1965. A Church of England view of the problem.
9. NOONAN, John T., *Contraception. A History of Its Treatment
by the Catholic Theologians and Canonists*. Cambridge,
Mass., Belknap Press, 1965.
10. WILLIAMS, Glanville, *The Sanctity of Life and the Criminal
Law*. New York, Alfred A. Knopf, Inc., 1966. A lawyer
assesses the legal and ethical problems.
11. WHELPTON, P. K., A. A. Campbell, and J. E. Patterson, *Fertility
and Family Planning in the United States*. Princeton,
Princeton University Press, 1966.
12. COOKE, Robert E., Andre E. Hellegers, Robert G. Hoyt, and
Herbert W. Richardson, *The Terrible Choice: The Abortion Dilemma*. New York, Bantam Books, 1968. Based on
the proceedings of the International Conference on Abortion sponsored by the Harvard Divinity School and the
Joseph P. Kennedy, Jr., Foundation, held in Washington,
D. C., in the fall of 1967.
13. AF GEIJERSTAM, Gunnar K. (ed.), *An Annotated Bibliography
of Induced Abortion*. Ann Arbor, Center for Population
Planning, University of Michigan, 1969. This volume, edited
by a Swedish obstetrician and gynecologist who is an expert

on the status of abortion in many parts of the world, contains thorough annotations on each of 1,175 recent publications on the problem. This is probably the most complete compendium of information on the subject now available.
14. PILPEL, Harriet F., and Kenneth P. Norwick, *When Should Abortion Be Legal? Public Affairs Pamphlet* No. 429, 1969.

Articles

15. TIETZE, C., "Abortion as a Cause of Death." *American Journal of Public Health,* 38 (1948), 1434.
* 16. HARDIN, G., "The History and Future of Birth Control." *Perspectives in Biology and Medicine* 10 (1966–67), 1.
17. HARDIN, G., "Blueprints, DNA, and Abortion: Scientific and Ethical Analysis." *Medical Opinion and Review,* February 1967, p. 74.
18. HARDIN, G., "Semantic Aspects of Abortion." *ETC: A Review of General Semantics,* 24 (September 1967), 263.
19. WISWANDER, K. R., M. Klein, and C. L. Randall, "Changing Attitudes Towards Therapeutic Abortions." *The Journal of the American Medical Association,* 196 (1966), 1140. Documentation of the privileged position of middle and upper class women in obtaining therapeutic abortions.
20. OBER, W. B., "We Should Legalize Abortion." *Saturday Evening Post,* October 8, 1966, p. 14. A doctor speaks for abortions.
* 21. LEDERBERG, Joshua, "A Geneticist Looks at Contraception and Abortion," in *The Changing Mores of Biomedical Research,* Ref. A 4. A Nobel Laureate looks at the problem from a biologist's point of view.
* 22. MEDAWAR, Sir Peter, "Discussion," in *The Changing Mores of Biomedical Research,* Ref. A 4, p. 61. A Nobel Laureate biologist discusses contraception and abortion.
23. KNUTSON, Andie L., "When Does a Human Life Begin? Viewpoints of Public Health Professionals." *American Journal of Public Health,* 57 (December 1967), 2163.
24. DAVIS, Kingsley, "Population Policy: Will Current Programs Succeed?" *Science,* 158 (November 10, 1967), 730. The efficacy is questioned of family planning programs that neglect the role of economic and cultural factors in motivation.

25. HARDIN, G., "Abortion—Or Compulsory Pregnancy?" *Journal of Marriage and the Family*, May 1968, p. 246.

26. GIANNELLA, D. A., "The Difficult Quest for a Truly Humane Abortion Law." *Villanova Law Review* 13 (Winter 1968), 257. A liberal Catholic discussion of the problem.

27. RYDER, N. B., and C. F. Westoff, "Fertility Planning Status of American Women 1965." Paper presented before Population Association of America, April 1968.

28. MEANS, Cyril C., Jr., "The Law of New York Concerning Abortion and the Status of the Foetus, 1664–1968: A Case of Cessation of Constitutionality." *New York Law Forum* 14 (Fall 1968), 411–515.

29. "The Desperate Dilemma of Abortion." *Time*, October 13, 1967, p. 32.

30. CAMPBELL, A. A., "The Role of Family Planning in the Reduction of Poverty." *Journal of Marriage and the Family*, 30 (1968), 236.

* 31. HARDIN, Garrett, "The Tragedy of the Commons." *Science*, 162 (December 13, 1968), 1243. An extremely important paper to the effect that the population problem has no technical solution, only a moral one based on "mutual coercion mutually agreed upon."

32. DYCK, Arthur J., "Why Contraceptive Programs Are Unsuccessful." *Harvard Divinity Bulletin*, Winter 1968, p. 6.

33. ELIOT, J. W., R. E. Hall, J. R. William, and C. Houser, "Therapeutic Abortion in Teaching Hospitals in the United States and Canada." *Proceedings of the International Conference on Abortion*, Hot Springs, Va., November 17–20, 1968.

34. "Abortion Experts, Saying Women Should Decide on Birth, Ask End to Curb," *The New York Times*, November 24, 1968.

35. LADER, Lawrence, "Non-Hospital Abortion." *Look*, January 21, 1969, p. 63.

36. BERELSON, Bernard, "Beyond Family Planning." *Science*, 163 (February 1969), 533. A comprehensive discussion of the compulsory measures that society may have to consider to solve the population problem.

37. BLAKE, Judith, "Population Policy for Americans: Is the Government Being Misled?" *Science*, 164 (May 2, 1969),

522. Birth control for the poor is not the answer; social institutions must be restructured to give to women creative opportunities other than childrearing.

38. HARKAVY, O., F. S. Jaffe, and S. M. Wishik, "Family Planning and Public Policy: Who Is Misleading Whom?" *Science,* 165 (July 25, 1969), 367.

* 39. PILPEL, Harriet, "The Right of Abortion." *Atlantic Monthly,* 223 (June 1969), 69. A spirited argument for liberalization, or better yet repeal, of all abortion laws to the end that population size may be controlled voluntarily, thus making coercive measures of imposed contraception or sterilization unnecessary.

* 40. TIETZE, C., and S. Lewit, "Abortion." *Scientific American,* 220 (January 1969), 21. An excellent review, written for the layman, of the current status and effects of abortion in the U. S. and especially in other countries where it has been legalized.

D. Religious and Ethical Principles

Books and Pamphlets

1. RAMSEY, Paul, *Deeds and Rules in Christian Ethics.* New York, Charles Scribner's Sons, 1967. A Protestant point of view.

2. McFADDEN, C. J., *Medical Ethics,* 6th ed. Philadelphia, F. A. Davis Co., 1967. A Catholic point of view.

3. FELDMAN, David M., *Birth Control and Jewish Law: Marital Relations, Contraception, and Abortion as Set Forth in the Classic Texts of Jewish Law.* New York, New York University Press, 1968. A Jewish point of view.

4. FLETCHER, Joseph, *Situation Ethics—The New Morality.* Philadelphia, Westminster Press, 1966. A prominent Protestant theologian discusses the new situation ethics that is based on love and individual decision-making rather than on dogma.

5. WATES, Wilson, *American Protestantism and Birth Control: An Examination of Shifts Within a Major Religious Value*

Orientation. Thesis, Harvard University, 1968. (Reviewed in *Harvard Theological Review,* October 1968.) This thesis shows a shift from opposition during 1870–1914 to acceptance during 1920–36.

Articles

6. KINSOLVING, L., "What About Therapeutic Abortion?" *The Christian Century,* 81 (May 13, 1964), 632.
7. HAYES, T. L., "Abortion I: A Biological View." *Commonweal,* March 17, 1967, p. 676.
8. BYRN, R. M., "Abortion II: A Legal View." *Commonweal,* March 17, 1967, p. 679.
9. NEHAUS, R. J., J. Pleasant, T. Wassmer, and A. E. Hellegers, "Abortion Beyond Assumptions." *Commonweal,* 86 (June 30, 1967), 408. The Catholic case against abortion.
10. HELLEGERS, A. E., "Critique of an Encyclical." *Medical Opinion and Review,* January 1969, p. 70. A noted Catholic obstetrician and gynecologist and member of the Papal Commission on Population and Birth Control criticizes the Pope's decision in *Humanae Vitae.*
11. BUSS, M. J., "The Beginning of Human Life as an Ethical Problem." *The Journal of Religion,* 47 (July 1967), 244.
12. RAMSEY, P., "The Sanctity of Life—In the First of It." *The Dublin Review,* Spring 1967, p. 1.
13. EASTMAN, N. J., "Induced Abortion and Contraception: A Consideration of Ethical Philosophy in Obstetrics." *Obstetrical and Gynecological Survey,* 22 (1967), 3.
14. CALDERONE, Mary S., "Sex, Religion, and Mental Health." *Journal of Religion and Health,* July 1967. The Executive Director of Sex Information and Education Council of the U. S. poses some hard questions that "science must dare to answer and religion must dare to free science to answer."
15. KIRKENDALL, Lester A., "Searching for the Roots of Moral Decisions." *The Humanist,* January–February 1967. "SIECUS's Director continues his probing analysis of his interpersonal relationships approach to moral decision making."
16. FLETCHER, J., and H. McCabe, "The New Morality." *Com-*

monweal, January 14, 1966, p. 427. The situational approach to sexual morality based on love meets the approach of the validity of absolutes.

E. Family Life

1. LOUKES, Harold, *Christians and Sex: A Quaker Comment.* London, Friends Home Service Committee, 1962. A thoughtful British Quaker presents the case for the traditional Christian morality of chastity and fidelity and the importance of subordinating sex to the total personal relationship—emotional, mental, and spiritual—between two human beings.
2. BARNES, Kenneth C., and others, *Towards a Quaker View of Sex: An Essay by a Group of Friends,* rev. ed. London, Friends Home Service Committee, 1964. A group of British Quaker educators, psychologists, psychiatrists, and a barrister, in undertaking to study the Quaker approach to homosexuality, found it necessary to encompass the whole field of sexual relationships. The result is a controversial but sincere, searching, and conscientious effort to find a new and deeper morality based not on external codes but on inner responsibility for the partner as a person. This book is more oriented to professional counseling, but like Harold Loukes's book (Ref. E 1), stresses the importance of preserving marriage and family life.
3. JOHNSON, Eric W., *Love and Sex in Plain Language.* Philadelphia, J. B. Lippincott Company, 1965. A Quaker educator discusses in simple language the problems facing sixth- to eighth-graders, who are just entering puberty.
4. GENNÉ, Elizabeth Stell, and William Henry Genné, *Foundations of Christian Family Policy.* New York, National Council of Churches of Christ, U. S. A., 1961. An account of the proceedings of the First North American Conference on Church and Family.
5. WYNN, John Charles (ed.), *Sex, Family, and Society in Theological Focus.* New York, Association Press, 1966. A group of essays by ten authors, dealing with some of the current issues that challenge the older ethic regarding sexual behavior and that demand a re-examination of the Christian

bases of decision making. This served as the preparatory study book for the Second North American Conference on Church and Family.

6. MACE, David R., *Marriage as Vocation: An Invitation to Relationship in Depth*. Philadelphia, Friends General Conference, 1969. A Friend, with extensive experience in marriage counseling, discusses various aspects of the new concept of marriage that emphasizes companionship rather than procreation.

7. SAGARIN, Edward (ed.), "Sex and the Contemporary Scene." *Annals of the American Academy of Political and Social Science*, Vol. 376 (March 1968). An entire issue devoted to essays on many aspects of the subject.

F. Genetic Counseling, Eugenics, and Genetic Engineering

Books and Pamphlets

1. ROSTAND, Jean, *Can Man Be Modified?*, trans. by J. Griffin. New York, Basic Books, Inc., 1959. A well-known French biologist discusses the biological future of man.

* 2. MEDAWAR, P. B., *The Future of Man*. London, Methuen and Co. Ltd.; New York, Basic Books, Inc., 1960. A series of brilliant lectures by a British biological scientist on the relative role of genetics and social factors in man's ongoing evolution.

* 3. MULLER, H. J., J. Lederberg, and others, in *Man and His Future*, Ref. A 2, pp. 247–298.

4. HALLER, Mark H., *Hereditarian Attitudes in American Thought*. New Brunswick, N. J., Rutgers University Press, 1963.

5. HUXLEY, Aldous, *Brave New World* and *Brave New World Revisited*. New York, Harper & Row, Publishers, 1965. Two famous books reprinted and reassessed by the author thirty-three years later and closer to the future.

6. SONNEBORN, T. M. (ed.), *The Control of Human Heredity and Evolution*. New York, The Macmillan Company, 1965.

* 7. ROSLANSKY, J. S. (ed.), *Genetics and the Future of Man. A Discussion at the First Nobel Conference.* New York, Appleton-Century-Crofts, Inc., 1966. Besides discussions of manipulating genetic change, eugenics, and the sociological aspects of genetic control, the chapter on the moral and religious implications by Dr. Paul Ramsey is especially to be noted.

8. FRAZER-ROBERTS, J. A., *Genetic Advice to Patients.* London, Oxford University Press, 1968.

* 9. OSBORN, Frederick, *The Future of Human Heredity: An Introduction to Eugenics in Modern Society.* New York, Weybright and Talley, Inc., 1968.

10. TAYLOR, Gordon Rattray, *The Biological Time Bomb.* Cleveland, The World Publishing Co., 1968. A detailed popular account by an able science writer of the potentialities for man in the fields of transplantation, mind manipulation, and genetic engineering.

11. ROSENFELD, Albert, *The Second Genesis: The Coming Control of Life.* Englewood Cliffs, N. J., Prentice-Hall, Inc., 1969. A dramatic, popular, and comprehensive exposition of the possibilities—and indeed the probabilities—of man's management of his own further evolution. For the layman by one of the chief science writers for *Life.*

12. *Genetic Counselling: Third Report of the WHO Expert Committee on Human Genetics.* World Health Organization Technical Report Series, No. 416. Geneva, 1969. An up-to-date analysis of genetic abnormalities on a world-wide basis. Indications and best techniques for the genetic counseling of individual couples are given. An annex provides a list of WHO reference centers concerned with human genetics or immunology. This report is summarized in *WHO Chronicle* 23 (July 1969), 318.

Articles

13. MULLER, Hermann J., "The Guidance of Human Evolution." *Perspectives in Biology and Medicine,* 3 (1959–60), 1. The chief advocate of sperm banks for eugenic improvement of the race states his case.

14. HUXLEY, Sir Julian, (a) "The Humanist Frame," in Sir Julian Huxley (ed.), *The Humanist Frame.* London, George Allen and Unwin Ltd., 1961, pp. 11–48; (b) "Eugenics in Evolu-

tionary Perspective." *Perspectives in Biology and Medicine,* 6 (1962–63), 155. The British biologist expounds his famous theory of evolutionary humanism with emphasis on the role of the psychosocial process.

15. ROBERTS, Catherine, "Positive Eugenics and Evolution." In Ref. A 7, Chap. 2. Also published as "Some Reflections on Positive Eugenics," *Perspectives in Biology and Medicine,* 7 (1963–64), 297. A humanistic microbiologist questions who is to decide which qualities are to be desired in the eugenically produced superior man of the future, and on what genes are located the coding for goodness, truth, and beauty.

16. MOTULSKY, A., and F. Hecht, "Genetic Prognosis and Counseling." *American Journal of Obstetrics and Gynecology,* 90 (1964), 1227.

17. NEEL, James V., "Some Genetic Aspects of Therapeutic Abortion." *Perspectives in Biology and Medicine,* 11 (1967–68), 129. A well-known American geneticist discusses the quantitative aspects of predicting genetic defects in unborn children, and its relation to eugenics.

18. GARDNER, Lytt I., "Genetic Counselling," in *Endocrine and Genetic Diseases of Childhood.* Philadelphia, W. B. Saunders Co., 1969, Chap. 22.

19. TURNER, John R. G., "How Does Treating Congenital Diseases Affect the Genetic Load?" *Eugenics Quarterly,* 15 (September 1968), 191. A mathematical and technical analysis showing that there are no grounds for ceasing to treat patients with genetic diseases, at least under present conditions.

20. INGLE, Dwight J., "Ethics of Genetic Intervention." *Medical Opinion and Review,* 3 (September 1967), 54–61. Good, sensible article, concluding that intervention with the biological endowment of man requires consent, freedom from government control, and guidance by physicians trained in human genetics.

* 21. HAMILTON, Michael, "New Life for Old: Genetic Decisions." *The Christian Century,* May 28, 1969. A thoughtful treatment of ethical and moral aspects by an Episcopal canon.

22. MATSUNAGA, E., "Measures Affecting Population Trends and Possible Genetic Consequences." World Population Conference, 1965, II, 481. New York, United Nations, 1967.

23. REINHOLD, Robert, "Evolution Control: A Genetic Advance." *The New York Times*, September 8, 1968.

24. REINHOLD, Robert, "Scientists Discuss Benefits of Genetic Manipulation." *The New York Times*, December 27, 1968.

G. Man's Control of Death

Books and Pamphlets

* 1. WOLSTENHOLME, G. E. W., and M. O'Connor (eds.), *Ethics in Medical Progress: With Special Reference to Transplantation,* a Ciba Foundation Symposium. Boston, Little, Brown and Company, 1966. Historically and intellectually one of the most important books on the subject. It is the record of a Ciba symposium held in London in 1966; the participants included many of the British, French, and American medical leaders in this field as well as a number of jurists, philosophers, theologians, and medical statesmen. The formal papers and the recorded discussions range widely over the many clinical, ethical, and legal aspects of the use of artificial and transplanted organs—both for acute resuscitation and chronic maintenance of life. The one criterion agreed upon was the worth of the human being and the quality of his life.

* 2. *Decisions about Life and Death. A Problem in Modern Medicine*. The Church Assembly Board for Social Responsibility. Church Information Office, London, 1965. Succinct statements by an anonymous group from the Church of England concerning the Church's approach to the problem of prolonging life in the dying patient: Life is the gift of God and should be maintained only as long as it is *human*.

3. "The Medical, Moral, and Legal Implications of Recent Medical Advances, A Symposium," *Villanova Law Review*, 13 (Summer 1968), 732–792. Discussion of primarily ethical problems involved in resuscitation and organ transplantation, by two physicians, two lawyers, a Jesuit priest, and a Protestant theologian.

4. HINTON, John, *The Dying Patient*. Baltimore, Penguin Books, Inc., 1967. A short book by a British physician.

5. SCHMECK, Harold M., *The Semi-Artificial Man.* New York, Walker and Company, 1965. A popular book written for the layman by an able science writer for *The New York Times.*

Articles

6. FLETCHER, J., "The Patient's Right To Die." *Harper's Magazine,* October 1960, p. 139.
7. AYD, F. J., Jr., "The Hopeless Case: Medical and Moral Considerations." *The Journal of the American Medical Association,* 181 (1962), 1099.
8. PLATT, R., "Reflections on Ageing and Death." *Lancet,* 1 (January 5, 1963), 1.
* 9. ARING, C. D., "Intimations of Mortality: An Appreciation of Death and Dying." *Annals of Internal Medicine,* 69 (July, 1968), 137.
10. WOODRUFF, M. F. A., "Ethical Problems in Organ Transplantation." *British Medical Journal,* 1 (1964), 1457.
11. ELKINTON, J. R., (a) "Moral Problems in the Use of Borrowed Organs, Artificial and Transplanted." *Annals of Internal Medicine,* 60 (1964), 309; (b) "Medicine and the Quality of Life." *Annals of Internal Medicine,* 64 (1966), 711; (c) "When Do We Let the Patient Die?" *Annals of Internal Medicine,* 68 (1968), 695.
12. LEAKE, C. D., "Technical Triumphs and Moral Muddles," in T. E. Starzl, *Experience in Renal Transplantation,* Philadelphia, W. B. Saunders Co., 1964, pp. 363–370; also in Ref. A 4, pp. 43–50.
13. MOORE, F. D., "Ethics in the New Medicine-Tissue Transplants." *The Nation,* April 5, 1965.
14. WILLIAMSON, W. P., "Life or Death—Whose Decision?" *The Journal of the American Medical Association,* 197 (1966), 793.
* 15. CLELAND, J. T. (ed.), "The Right to Live and the Right to Die." *Medical Times,* 95 (November 1967), 1171.
16. STARZL, T. E., "Ethical Problems in Organ Transplantation: A Clinician's Point of View." In Ref. A 4, pp. 32–36.
17. (a) BIÖRCK, G., "On the Definitions of Death." *World Medical Journal,* 14 (1967), 137. (b) MULLER, P.-H., "Legal Med-

icine and the Delimitation of Death." *World Medical Journal,* 14 (1967), 140. (c) VOIGHT, J., "The Criteria of Death, Particularly in Relation to Transplantation Surgery." *World Medical Journal,* 14 (1967), 143. (d) WASSERMAN, H. P., "Problematical Aspects of the Phenomenon of Death." *World Medical Journal,* 14 (1967), 146.

* 18. BIÖRCK, G., "Thoughts on Life and Death." *Perspectives in Biology and Medicine,* 11 (1967–68), 527.

   19. FLETCHER, G. P., "Legal Aspects of the Decision Not To Prolong Life." *The Journal of the American Medical Association,* 203 (1968), 65.

   20. LEWIN, W., "Severe Head Injuries," in Ref. A 5, p. 1208.

   21. BEECHER, H. K., "Ethical Problems Created by the Hopelessly Unconscious Patient." *New England Journal of Medicine,* 278 (June 27, 1968), 1425.

* 22. "A Definition of Irreversible Coma." Report of the Ad Hoc Committee of the Harvard Medical School To Examine the Definition of Brain Death. *The Journal of the American Medical Association,* 205 (August 5, 1968), 337. The most authoritative and definitive statement to date on the medical criteria for death of the brain.

   23. BLUEMLE, L. W., Jr., "The Current Status of Chronic Hemodialysis." *The American Journal of Medicine,* 44 (1968), 749.

   24. *Report of the Committee on Chronic Renal Disease,* C. W. Gottschalk, Chairman. Washington, D. C., U. S. Bureau of the Budget, September 1967.

   25. MOORE, F. D., G. E. Burch, D. E. Harken, H. J. C. Swan, J. E. Murray, and C. W. Lillihei, "Cardiac and Other Organ Transplantation: In the Setting of Transplant Science as a National Effort." Report of the Fifth Bethesda Conference of the American College of Cardiology, September 28–29, 1968. *The Journal of the American Medical Association,* 206 (December 9, 1968), 2489.

* 26. PAGE, I. H., "The Ethics of Heart Transplantation." *The Journal of the American Medical Association,* 207 (January 6, 1969), 109. An extremely thoughtful and penetrating analysis by an outstanding medical scientist, editor, and statesman.

   27. SADLER, A. M., Jr., B. L. Sadler, and E. B. Stason, "The Uni-

form Anatomical Gift Act. A Model for Reform." *The Journal of the American Medical Association*, 206 (December 9, 1968), 2501. This model law for the legal granting of human tissues and organs is summarized in Appendix VII.

28. *Use of Human Tissues and Organs for Therapeutic Purposes: A Survey of Existing Legislation.* Geneva, World Health Organization, 1969. Comprehensive WHO Report on the legal status of tissue and organ transplants in various countries of the world.

29. MOORE, F. D., "Medical Responsibility for the Prolongation of Life." *The Journal of the American Medical Association*, 206 (October 7, 1968), 384.

30. COLLINS, V. J., "Limits of Medical Responsibility in Prolonging Life: Guides to Decisions." *The Journal of the American Medical Association*, 206 (October 7, 1968), 389.

H. Experimentation on Humans

Although this subject was not discussed directly in this book, it is closely related to the over-all problem of the impact of biomedical science on human life. For those who might be interested, a short bibliography of this particular subject follows.

Books

1. LADIMER, I., and R. W. Newman (eds.), *Clinical Investigation in Medicine: Legal, Ethical and Moral Aspects. An Anthology and Bibliography.* Boston, Law-Medicine Research Institute, Boston University, 1963.

2. GRAUBARD, S. R. (ed.), *Ethical Aspects of Experimentation with Human Subjects. Daedalus*, Spring, 1969. A wide-ranging set of essays on all aspects of the subject by knowledgeable physicians, lawyers, a philosopher, a sociologist, and an anthropologist.

Articles

3. MCCANCE, R. A., "The Practice of Experimental Medicine."

Proceedings of the Royal Society of Medicine, 44 (1950), 189.

4. FREUND, P. A., "Ethical Problems in Human Experimentation." *New England Journal of Medicine*, 273 (1965), 687.

5. STUMPF, S. E., "Some Moral Dimensions of Medicine." *Annals of Internal Medicine*, 64 (1966), 460.

6. BEECHER, H. K., "Ethics and Clinical Research." *New England Journal of Medicine*, 274 (1966), 1354.

7. ELKINTON, J. R., "The Experimental Use of Human Beings" (editorial). *Annals of Internal Medicine*, 65 (1966), 371.

8. SCHREINER, G. E., "The Ethics of Human Experimentation." *The Pharos*, 29 (1966), 78.

I. Science, the Human Condition, and the Future

1. WHITEHEAD, Alfred North, *Science and the Modern World*. New York, The Macmillan Co. and Cambridge University Press, 1925. The late mathematician and philosopher presents brilliantly, but with a high degree of abstraction and conceptual thinking, his view of the place of science in society and its relation to religion.

2. EDDINGTON, Sir Arthur, *Science and the Unseen World*. New York, The Macmillan Company, 1929. The late astronomer and astrophysicist of the University of Cambridge was one of the first scientists to apply Einstein's theory of relativity to the interpretation of the nature of the physical world. He was also a member of the Society of Friends, and in this lucid essay he tells how, to him the principles of science, based on mathematical symbols limited to the world of space and time, are yet consonant with his faith in a world of the spirit based on the symbols of human personality.

3. EISELEY, Loren, *The Immense Journey*. New York, Random House, 1946. "An imaginative naturalist explores the mysteries of man and nature." A series of beautifully written essays by a biologist-anthropologist who manages to capture the nuances of the dilemma of the human spirit in specific experiences that also reveal the long perspective of the evolution of life.

4. MUMFORD, Lewis, *The Transformations of Man*. New York, Harper & Row, Publishers, 1956; New York, Collier Books, 1962. A well-known social critic examines the various stages of human development and the prospects for a future "One World man" who will realize the full potentialities of human creativity and spiritual energy.

5. BRONOWSKI, J., *Science and Human Values*. Hammondsworth, Penguin Books Ltd., 1958. A provocative British scientist finds that science contributes to the values of truth and integrity and hence of human dignity.

6. BERRILL, N. J., *You and the Universe*. New York, Dodd, Mead & Company, 1957; London, Dennis Dobson, 1959. The well-known biologist and humanist, introduced in Ref. A 8, tells in simple language the story of the evolution of the universe and of life on earth. That man, with his conscious mind, comes from stardust and is a part of the mystery, "should give us faith in our significance."

* 7. HUXLEY, Sir Julian (ed.), *The Humanist Frame*. London, George Allen and Unwin Ltd., 1961. The opening essay by Sir Julian has already been cited as Ref. F 14. The rest of the book consists of a series of stimulating essays by humanist thinkers who examine a multitude of facets of the human condition from the point of view of their respective fields. Especially recommended are the essays: "The New Medicine and Its Responsibilities" by Sir Robert Platt, "What Are People For?" by G. C. L. Bertram, and "Human Potentialities" by Aldous Huxley.

8. LONSDALE, Dame Kathleen, (a) "Science and Ethics." *Nature*, January 20, 1962, p. 209; (b) "Science and the Good Life." *Advancement of Science*, September 1968, p. 1. Another eminent British scientist—a crystallographer—and a member of the Society of Friends explores the social responsibility of science that stems from its growing power. The second paper is Dame Kathleen's Presidential Address to the British Association for the Advancement of Science, of which organization she is the first woman to be president.

9. ROBERTS, Catherine, *The Scientific Conscience*, Ref. A 7. Included again here because of the author's concern over the failure of science to recognize its limitations and its responsibilities to foster human values.

* 10. BOULDING, Kenneth E., *The Meaning of the 20th Century. The Great Transition.* New York, Harper & Row, Publishers, 1965. Here is a lucid, perceptive, and cogent analysis by a Quaker economist of the central problems of the human race today. The impact of science on today's society is forcing a transition from civilization to a technological age of "post-civilization." The traps besetting an orderly transition are many: war, difficulties of economic development, overpopulation (licenses to have babies may yet become necessary), exhaustion of natural resources, and irreversible pollution of the environment. He analyzes the roles of ideologies and the methods of resolving conflicts, and ends on a note of cautious and critical acceptance of the transitions, seeing hope in the "invisible college" of people all over the world who recognize the nature of this current transition and who by changing "from the unexamined to the examined life" are "contributing towards its successful fulfillment." This is an important book, one that is easy to read and hard to put down.

11. PLATT, John Rader, *The Step to Man.* New York, John Wiley & Sons, Inc., 1966. This is a collection of essays by a philosophical physicist who is interested in social dynamics and the role of "chain reactions" in changing society. The volume takes its title from the last essay, first published in *Science*, 149 (August 6, 1965), 607; in this essay he predicts that if mankind can adapt to the rapid changes of scientific technology and survive during the next twenty years, a long plateau of a stable population and a better quality of life is probable.

12. DUBOS, René, *Man Adapting.* New Haven, Yale University Press, 1965. A distinguished microbiologist and medical philosopher discusses the paradox that man's almost unlimited technical power in medicine is limited by social and economic factors. Health or disease is the expression of his success or failure in adapting to his environment. This book is a penetrating and detailed analysis of the biological and social implications of this adaptation.

Members of the Working Party on *Who Shall Live?*

HENRY J. CADBURY, Ph.D. Emeritus Professor of Divinity, Harvard University; author of books and articles on Biblical subjects and on Quakerism; Fellow, American Academy of Arts and Sciences; member, American Philosophical Society and Central Philadelphia Monthly Meeting of the Religious Society of Friends; Chairman, Board of Directors of the AFSC, 1921–34, 1944–60, and Honorary Chairman since 1960.

LORRAINE K. CLEVELAND, M.S.W. Director, AFSC Family Planning Program; administrative assignments with the AFSC in the United States and overseas since 1944; staff member, family and child welfare agencies in Illinois, Kansas, Louisiana, and Oklahoma; Assistant State Director of Public Welfare, Oklahoma (1939–44); member, Newtown Monthly Meeting of the Religious Society of Friends.

JOHN C. COBB, M.D., M.P.H. Professor and Chairman, Department of Preventive Medicine and Comprehensive Health Care, University of Colorado; Area Consultant on Maternal

137

and Child Health, Division of Indian Health, United States Public Health Service (1956–60); Director, Medical-Social Research Project on Population in Pakistan (1960–64); certified by the American Board of Preventive Medicine; Fellow of the American Public Health Association; member, Board of Directors of American Association of Planned Parenthood Physicians, Friends Medical Society, and Executive Committee for the Colorado Area Office of the AFSC.

ELIZABETH CONARD CORKEY, M.D., M.P.H.   Family Planning Consultant, Mecklenburg County Health Department, Charlotte, North Carolina; Associate Professor of Obstetrics, Women's Christian Medical College, Shanghai (1932–35); medical missionary in China (1935–46); Assistant Health Director, Wayne and Green Counties, North Carolina (1948–55); Assistant Health Director and Medical Director of Family Planning Clinic, Mecklenburg County Health Department (1955–68); certified by the American Board of Preventive Medicine; Fellow of the American College of Preventive Medicine; member, American Association of Planned Parenthood Physicians, Committee on Population and Family Planning of the Maternal and Child Health Section of the American Public Health Association (Chairman, 1967–68), American School Health Association, Friends Medical Society, and Charlotte Monthly Meeting of the Religious Society of Friends.

RICHARD L. DAY, M.D.   Professor of Pediatrics, Mount Sinai School of Medicine, City University of New York; Chief of Pediatric Service, King's County Hospital, New York (1953–60); Professor of Pediatrics, State University of New York (1953–60); Professor of Pediatrics, University of Pittsburgh (1960–65); Medical Director and Chief of Staff, Children's Hospital of Pittsburgh (1960–65); Medical Director, Planned Parenthood—World Population (1965–67); certified by the American Board of Pediatrics; member, American Board of Pediatrics (President, 1964–65), Editorial Board of *American*

Journal of Diseases of Children (Chief Editor, 1958–60), American Pediatric Society (President, 1969–70), Friends Medical Society, Scarsdale Monthly Meeting of the Religious Society of Friends.

JOHAN W. ELIOT, M.D., M.S. in Pediatrics, M.P.H. Associate Professor of Population Planning, University of Michigan School of Public Health; Consultant on Maternal and Child Health and Family Planning for AFSC programs in Algeria and Togo; Pediatric Consultant (including direction of center for evaluation of retarded children), Arkansas State Board of Health (1952–58); Pediatric Consultant, Michigan Department of Health (1958–64); certified by the American Board of Pediatrics and by the American Board of Preventive Medicine; member, Committee on Population and Family Planning of the Maternal and Child Health Section of the American Public Health Association (Chairman, 1964–67), Board of Directors of Planned Parenthood—World Population, Friends Medical Society, Ann Arbor Monthly Meeting of the Religious Society of Friends.

J. RUSSELL ELKINTON, M.D. Editor, *Annals of Internal Medicine*; Professor of Medicine and formerly the Chief of the Chemical Section, Department of Medicine, University of Pennsylvania School of Medicine; Staff Physician, Hospital of the University of Pennsylvania; Diplomate, American Board of Internal Medicine; Fellow of the American College of Physicians and of the Royal College of Physicians of London; member, American Society for Clinical Investigation, Association of American Physicians, Elwyn Institute for the mentally retarded (Board of Directors, 1956–68, and Chairman of Medical Committee, 1960–67), Friends Medical Society (Chairman since 1966), Media Monthly Meeting of the Religious Society of Friends.

JOSEPH STOKES, JR., M.D. Emeritus Professor of Pediatrics, University of Pennsylvania; Chairman of Committee on Family Planning of the AFSC (since 1964); Physician in Chief, Children's Hospital of Philadelphia (1939–63); Director, Commission on Measles and Mumps, Board for the Investigation and Control of Epidemic Diseases (1942–46); certified by the American Board of Pediatrics; member, American Academy of Pediatrics, American Pediatric Society (President, 1958–59), Association of American Physicians, Society of American Microbiologists, Society for Pediatric Research (one of the founders and past President), American Philosophical Society, Board of Managers of Haverford College, of Wistar Institute, and of The Woods Schools, Friends Medical Society (Chairman, 1952–55, Executive Secretary since 1966), Germantown Monthly Meeting of the Religious Society of Friends.

Index